The Me Disease

A Spiritual Journey from me to We

Melissa H. Thompson

© 2019 Melissa Thompson

All rights reserved. No part of this publication may be reproduced, distributed, or transmitted in any form or by any means, including photocopying, recording, or other electronic or mechanical methods, without the prior written permission of the publisher, except in the case of brief quotations embodied in reviews and certain other non-commercial uses permitted by copyright law.

Praise for "The Me Disease"

In her lively, accessible book, so timely in our I/me/mine culture, Melissa Thompson charts a path for us toward a lighter, freer, more joyful life. Highly commended.

Dr. James Howell, *Senior Pastor, Myers Park United Methodist Church, Charlotte, NC, and author of 20 books, most recently "Birth: The Mystery of Being Born"*

"Just one more chapter!" is how I felt reading this compelling study of our own self-centered ways. This gem draws you in with truth in love and will not let you stay where you started! Whether used in a group study or a private reflection on your own "Me Disease" you will be transformed by the gentle yet powerful message. Cannot wait for the next one by this talented author!

Bonnie Burkett, *author of "ENOUGH! The College Cost Crisis"*

Living in your truth and trusting in God is the most real gem in life. In her first debut book, Author Melissa Thompson shares her life's journey filled with joy, laughter, and undeniable strength. "The Me Disease" will ground you with compelling self-reflection and give you hope towards having a better God-giving life.

Kathy B., *CEO-President Source Radio Network/SRN Live Television*

When a well-meaning life is upside down, reorienting can be an adventure! In this powerful testament to the spirit, mind, and body connection, Melissa H. Thompson offers us a vulnerable account of the journey that altered her relationships, career, spirituality, health, and ego. Then, with compassionate encouragement and plenty of great resources, she invites us to take our own journey to a life that is closer to God, community, and to the true self we were born to be. A powerful delight!

***Jeff Albert**, sculptor, writer, and workshop leader*

Do you live from your true self? How do you connect to this person and begin to live from your true self: the person God created you to be? The good news is your true self is not an endpoint. It is a continuous journey that God will take you on when you let go and trust. Melissa serves as our guide as she shares her journey from her false self to her true self and what she did to stay faithful to this path. Highly recommended!

***Rich Lewis**, author of "Sitting with God: A Journey to Your True Self Through Centering Prayer"*

*This is my first fruits offering.
I hope it serves to be authentic of who I am
and who I am becoming.
To be true to the God I experience daily,
as Christ continues to reveal the Holy Spirit in me.
And above all else, to God be the glory.
-M*

Letter from My Husband

Melissa,

You are going to knock people's socks off with this book. Especially the people who know you. Everyone who knows you has always considered you a spiritual leader. Especially in our "group." But nobody really knows the leg work, time and energy you have put into being YOU. This book opens the door and gives everyone a peek at what your life, outside of their presence, is really like. With that, you are giving a roadmap to everyone. A roadmap that will lead anyone who chooses to follow, down a knowledge-filled, full of God's Grace and Love, road. Sure, they will find the pot holes just like you have. When they do, they can look back to this and figure out how to get through them. You have laid it out for them. You have led by example!! I love you and am so proud of you.

-Trav

TABLE OF CONTENTS

Introduction	1
Chapter One: My Physical, Mental, and Spiritual Collision	11
Chapter Two: Little Signs	25
Chapter Three: Where it all Began: The Symptoms	37
Chapter Four: The Uncovering—The Shift from Big ME to Little Me	51
Chapter Five: The Shredding of Self	63
Chapter Six: Lessons Learned	77
Chapter Seven: The True Self Emerges	89
Chapter Eight: Becoming the Disciple—The Shift from Me to WE	99
Chapter Nine: Meeting Together—The "We" Emerges	117
Chapter Ten: Mentor/Mentee—Better Together—Me2We	131
Chapter Eleven: Sanctification—Holiness—Perfecting Christ in Us	145
Chapter Twelve: We are ONE—The Joy of Community	159

Introduction

PEOPLE ASK ME ALL THE time what my book is about. The book is entitled, *The Me Disease* and I am convinced we all have it. The world teaches us to cover up who we really are, and this book describes my journey back to who God created me to be, the "God-created self" who has always been there from the very beginning. That's the short of it. But for me, the journey has been so very long. It jump-started about seven years ago when my husband and I went on a weekend spiritual retreat called The Walk to Emmaus. The men attend the first weekend followed by the women going the next. My husband anxiously awaited my return home eager to hear about my experience after the women's weekend. No sooner than I walked through the door, he asked me, "So . . . what'd you think?" I quickly blurted out, "God said we need to sell our house!" Stunned and befuddled, he replied, "God didn't tell me that!" That's how our journey began. One act of obedience followed by another act of obedience, leading us to the very place we find ourselves today.

Hearing from God and responding to His wishes set us on a journey. After about two and a half years, we did sell our house. Then, God asked us to leave our community and the church I grew up in. A couple of years later, God asked us to sell my business to follow my dream of writing a book. This is that book. But my dream of writing a book is so singular when the dream God has for my life is very much plural. So, here we are, off and running, uncertain where we are going or when we will get there.

My family and I are at the beginning of this journey and anxious to see where this path takes us. It's a weird feeling, journeying along not really knowing where you are going. Often when you set out on a path, like a nature trail, you have a destination in mind. You know where you are going and how long it will take to get there. I remember, years ago, being on a field trip with my son to the natural science center. Our guide led us on an easy walking trail for the group. As we meandered along, the path became worn. With no directional signs to tell us which way to go or how much farther, I became nervous. I had no idea where we were. The guide, however, seemed confident, as if he had been this way many times before. Perhaps he had. It was his job. But I had not.

Anxiously, I searched for clues that might indicate how much farther we were going. I had no choice but to trust my guide. As we took many turns, questions kept popping in my head. "Where are we going?" and "How long until we get there?" He smiled at me, sensing my apprehension. I had to trust him. However, the kids were mesmerized by the crunchy sound of the leaves that covered the ground and a rotting log that housed roly-polies and other creepy crawlies just underneath it in the moist, dark soil. They didn't care if they were on the right path or if they were even on a path. Fascinated by the buzzing of the bees and the chirping of the birds, their eyes remained wide open with anticipation of each new discovery. They were not even concerned with the guide, only that they follow him. I didn't have time to notice the bugs. I was too busy being concerned with what I didn't know. I still long for that childlike trust on my life's path, so that I, too, can enjoy the journey I have found myself on. I often ask, "God, help me to trust you like these little children."

As the way opened before us, we found ourselves at the top of the most beautiful overlook. The foliage of reds, orange, greens, and browns scattered the treetops and gave way to the mountainous view of blue sky and fluffy white clouds. It was spectacular. I inhaled the deepest, freshest breath of cool air and released it ever so gently. Intuitively, I knew that it is not just about me and my experience. This world is too big to be just about me. It is about us, all of us. We are part of something bigger than ourselves. And when I glimpse the greatest of creation, I am reminded of this.

Thinking back, I often find myself asking God the same questions I wanted to ask the guide. "Where are we going?" and "How long until we get there?" God's reply is always the same, "Trust me." I struggle with being on a path and not being there yet. I wonder what is up ahead and how much longer until I get there. When I get caught up in the questions, I miss the beauty around me. I miss the path itself. I miss God. I pray that God will teach me to trust HIM completely. I know there is a spectacular view just up ahead. But even still, there is so much to experience right here along the way. All I need to do is stop worrying and trust God.

I remember when God first said, "Sell the house" and then a few years later, "Leave the church." We had no idea God was setting the stage for us to be able to make the dream of writing a book our reality. God is always at work, and scripture tells us, "working for the good of those that love God[1]." Even when we cannot see it, God is still working. At this time, we had no idea what God was up to. We only knew what God asked us to do, and, in an act of obedience, we attempted to fulfill those tasks, one request at a time. I love how the Message says it in Romans 8:28, "We can be sure that every detail in our lives of love for God is worked into something good. God knew what he was doing from the

---

[1] Romans 8:28 Zondervan NIV Study Bible

THE ME DISEASE

very beginning.[2]" That realization gives me so much peace. God knows what God is doing. This means that I don't have to know what God is doing. I only need to trust God. I wish I could stay here in the security this knowledge provides, but my earthly brain wants to rationalize life. God cannot be rationalized. God is God. The Alpha and the Omega[3]. The beginning and the end. It's too much for my feeble brain to fathom.

In my journey of discovering who God is and who God created me to be, God led me and my family to the realization of *The Me Disease*. As we continue to walk the path God has set before us, we continue to move into that reality of who we were created to be, longing to be wherever it is we are going, I am faced with lesson after lesson. I am learning to trust my Guide and enjoy the journey. These are important lessons and, with each step I take, I am one step closer to becoming who God created me to be.

I hope this captivates you, but what I really hope is that you see God in my life and thus how real God is in yours as well. If this book does nothing more than show you the reality of who God is to me, and how real God can be to you, then it will have done its job.

This is an invitation for you come along with me on this journey. I'm not there yet. As we go, there will be questions for you, the same questions I am asking myself. The book is interactive by design. Because, well, God is interactive. God is not a God that sits far away in heaven waiting to see if we will say the right prayers and do the right things. No. God wants to meet you here, today, right where you are. I hope my stories will help

---

[2] Romans 8:28 The Message; Eugene Peterson – Nothing beats my go to favorite Bible. It's marked up and highlighted. Well worn to say the least. However, I have found it extremely useful to read other version and it often gives me a glimpse of something I might have missed in the familiarity of my own.
[3] Revelation 22:13 NIV

you find God in your life. Because God is indeed in your life whether you realize it or not. God is already here.

Before we go any further, I want to share two back stories with you. The first revolves around my breakdown. Yes, I said breakdown. I'll tell you all about it in the chapters to follow. One day, I found myself alone in a quiet house watching Oprah's Super Soul Sunday[4]. My husband was at the fire station where he works as a full-time fire captain. My son was at a sleepover. Oprah was interviewing Jack Canfield, the author of *Chicken Soup for the Soul*[5]. Jack was mid-sentence when I turned on the program. He said, "If you have a dream, it is not your dream, but God's dream for your life. And if it is God's dream for your life, God will give you everything you need to fulfill that dream."[6] Chills ran down my spine, and something inside me shifted. Immediately, I was flooded with joy, even though I was unsure why. It was strange.

My dream of writing a book came to mind. I had not thought of it in ages. Back in college, I took several creative writing classes and fantasized about the first book I would write. I never let go of the idea of writing a book. Over the years, I gathered ideas and random thoughts for no less than 12 potential books. Up until that day, I had possessed the dream, clutching it with a clenched fist, holding it so tight that I was strangling the life out of it. When I heard Jack, I instantly knew it was not my dream to possess. This was God's dream for my life. I envisioned myself opening my hands, arms raised, and releasing that dream. Out of my hands flew a handful of beautiful blue butterflies. I watched as they fluttered up, up, and away.

---

[4] Oprah's Super Soul Sunday Episode with Jack Canfield, best-selling author of *Chicken Soup for the Soul*, show aired December 15, 2015.
[5] Jack Canfield, Chicken Soup for the Soul
[6] Quote from Jack Canfield

THE ME DISEASE

Illustration by Grace Gainey

In that moment, I confessed to God my possessiveness of this dream and surrendered that dream to God. More joy flooded my senses. Just then, God spoke to my heart, "Sell your business and do this thing." Even today, I hear it so clearly. I knew 'this thing' was to write this book. Well, I didn't know it was this book, but I knew it was to sell my business and chase after my dream of writing a book.

Excited, I reached for my cell phone to call my husband. I knew when Travis answered, he had the power to breathe life or death into this dream just by his response. Nervously, I waited for him to pick up the phone, excited to share all that I had experienced. I recounted every detail from Jack on *Oprah*, to Jack's words, my joy, the vision of releasing the dream, and then God's words to me. Holding my breath, I paused in expectation of his response. Imagine my surprise when he blurted out, with the same level of excitement, "Let's do it!" It brings tears to my eyes today just thinking about it. On that day, between Jack and Oprah, me and God, and then me and my husband, that dream took flight just like those butterflies, and it is still lifting today. It is an exciting time even though I have this strange feeling we are only at the beginning.

I tell you these things to set the stage for this book, *The Me Disease*. God speaks to me and can speak to you, too. My prayer is that these stories will give testimony to the reality of God in my life. That somehow my stories will lead you to a place where you realize God can be that real in yours. That's what this is about. God does, in fact, speak to everyday average folk like me. And if God can speak to me, God can speak to you. By sharing my stories, I hope to show you how to hear from God.

The second story is the birth of this book itself. I was so excited about the call of obedience to "sell my business and write the book." But I had no idea which book I would write. I scoured through my journals and notebooks, looking for that one book idea. I carefully pondered all my notes, thoughts, titles, and pieces of paragraphs held together in my pink three-ring binder, just waiting for me. God had given me the green light. I felt this urgency to begin but had no idea where to start. I began praying about the book I was supposed to write.

One morning, several weeks later, I was standing in front of the bathroom mirror, getting ready for work. As I applied my charcoal eyeliner, I thought about Jack's words[7] and God's instructions[8]. I sensed

---

[7] Jack Canfield said, "if you have a dream, it is not your dream. It is God's dream for your life. And if it is God's dream for your life, then God has already given you everything you need to fulfill that dream. You would have never even had the dream to start with if you were not already equipped to fulfill it.

[8] God said, "Sell the business and do this thing." – Advice: if you think you are hearing from God, write it down. If it is God, God will confirm it through other people, songs and scripture.

that this could be the start of something big. As I leaned forward, peering into the mirror, God let me see the future. I saw the book, the title, the colors, and the design. I even saw the twelve[9] chapter titles. This is that book, the very one you hold in your hands today.

Immediately, I rushed to my computer, knowing I only had a small window of time before all those thoughts would vanish like vapor. Attempting to capture the moment, I typed up every detail. I have had experiences like this before. These "God moments" can disappear as fast as they arrive. I looked at my computer in amazement. There it was, the book, handed to me by God Himself. In the days to follow, God would continue to hand me pieces of this book. God gave me my starting place. I was off and running.

So, I have told you about my dream and about the birth of the book. Let me tell you a little about the book itself. I believe *The Me Disease* is a real illness. I also believe we all have it. I can write this book because I've had this disease probably all my life. If you think you don't, be aware. You may be more infected than you think! This disease has been around so long that we don't even recognize it as a condition anymore. We just accept it as part of who we are. It is NOT who we are. It is not who we have been created to be. We must remember who we are and who we were created to be. If you don't know who you are or who you were created to be, read on. We will unpack this together.

Through my own experiences, we will go through the signs and symptoms of this disease. You can decide for yourself if you have it and to what extent. However, this is my story of self-discovery and transformation. Everyone is different, yet in our core, in our soul, we are one. For me, my awakening came in the manifestation of sickness. From that illness, I was forced to take a long, hard look at my life, my real life.

---

[9] There is significance in the number 12. Twelve represents wholeness and completeness.

Not the life that I let the world see, but what was really going on. There were things happening in my marriage that I had been ignoring for years, boundary issues within my family, and possessiveness of my church. I was trying to be a business owner, wife, mother, and servant of God. All the while, I was unknowingly becoming a slave to myself and the church. My life was out of balance. God has a way of waking us up when the life *we* created is not the life God created for us.

Unbeknownst to me, my world was upside down and inside out. These are my awful, scary truths. You probably have some of your own when you think about it. Our pasts can serve a purpose in bringing us to the present moment. If we will learn from our past mistakes, they will equip us for all that awaits us in the future. We can be our best self, our true self, the self that God created us to be.

I began asking questions, questions I am still asking today. And those questions have been included in each chapter. It is okay to ask questions. More importantly, it is alright to not know the answers. God wants all your questions. I would invite you to meet me in the pages of this book. In meeting me here, I hope you meet yourself as well. You see, me and you, we are one. We are the same. Created by the same Maker. If I bear my ugly truth to you, would you be so brave to bear yours? For our Creator knows it all and is waiting to embrace you as you are.

God can set you free from the life you have created for yourself, that busy, hectic, frenzied life that we all seem to have. We think that if we busy ourselves enough, we won't have to acknowledge the emptiness that is ever present in our lives. We think that if we move fast enough, no one will notice who we really are, that no one will see the pain that we carry with us. However, we were made for community. I want to stand with you. I want to encourage, support, and guide you. There are lessons to be learned, and they are best learned together. My prayer is that you learn from me and my mistakes. I want to help you realize that God can transform you into your best self. Your God-created self that is buried deep inside you. I will show you how to stop hiding who you are. When you hide who you are, you hide who we all are, the essence of the soul, not just mine, but ours. When I reveal the truth of who I have been created to be, I hope it will encourage you to do the same.

The beautiful thing is that if you are holding this book right now, it's because you are ready. God knows you are ready. And way down deep inside, you know you are ready, too. You are ready for more of God and more of who God created you to be. It's the missing piece. It's the void and the emptiness that you feel. That's why you are here. You, my friend, are right where you are supposed to be. Start paying attention. God is speaking to you. This book in your hands is proof God is already speaking into your life. Come with me and let's walk this path together, trusting that we don't have to know where we are going or when we will get there. Trusting that God is with us. All we have to do is trust God. God has something wonderful to show you. The funny thing is that "something" is *you*. The real you. The you that you were created to be.

—Melissa

Chapter One

My Physical, Mental, and Spiritual Collision

IT SEEMS TO ME THAT the hardest times in my life are the times when I learned the most. These are the times when everything is falling apart around me, and I am holding on for dear life. Funny how often, when you are in it, you don't even realize what is going on around you. When I look back on one of the darkest times in my life, I find God right there with me. Ironically, at the time, I felt the furthest from God. In fact, I was convinced that God had abandoned me when I needed Him most. Me, God's faithful servant, now laid up in the bed, and God was nowhere to be found. I had too many of my own personal experiences of God to question His existence. But where was He when I needed Him most?

Here's what happened. I had a complete breakdown. A collision of sorts. My father likes to refer to it as my "medical crisis." There is so much stigma around the term "breakdown." But it really is the best word to describe what happened to me. I had a physical, mental, and spiritual collision. All systems malfunctioned. The symptoms began manifesting as migraines with a twist of vertigo, neither of which had I experienced before. I had light and sound sensitivity mixed with dizziness. It was

THE ME DISEASE

difficult to stand upright, and I often found myself clinging to chairs, tables, or the wall to stabilize me. Walking was challenging; therefore, driving was out of the question. Initially, the doctors thought I had a brain tumor. I thought I had a brain tumor. My husband thought I had a brain tumor. My mother would not utter the words "brain tumor" for fear of the power of our words.

The day it all began, I had what can only be described as a "vision flip." My nephew and I were preparing to order our usual at our favorite sushi restaurant when my line of sight flipped upside down and then right side up. Dizzy and a little flustered, I noticed my hands began to tingle. I dismissed it as a fluke, and we went on with our meal. Afterward, I headed back to the office, still aware of the tingling in my hands.

A couple of days later, while driving my son to my mom's house, I glanced off the road at a house on a hill. Unclear as to what really happened, my eyes locked on the house and lingered there for longer than I realized. I was in slow motion, like being in a trance. The blaring of a car horn brought me back to reality. My car had drifted over the yellow line into oncoming traffic. Frantically, I jerked the steering wheel to the right to avoid a head-on collision. My heart was racing as I pulled the car to a complete stop at the intersection. With tears in my eyes, I glanced over at my son. He looked back at me with amazement at our near miss and at the tears rolling down my face. I'm not sure he had ever seen me cry before. I wiped the tears from my cheeks as I began to sort through what had just happened. The realization that we could have just died began to sink into my bones. This and the fact that something might be wrong with me.

I could feel the delay in my brain, the tingling in my hands, and the rush of the unknown waiting for me just up ahead. I had no idea of the darkness these things would bring with them.

I slowly proceeded to my mom's house to drop my son off and went on to work, trying to ignore all the symptoms I was beginning to feel. I attempted to type an email, but my computer screen quivered, making it hard to focus. Nauseated and nervous, I decided to go to the doctor to find out what was going on. I had way too much work to do to be slowed down by whatever this was.

Mentally, I began preparing for the worst: a brain tumor. The doctor did a quick exam, and, believing I showed signs of a brain tumor as well, sent me straight to the emergency room for a CAT scan. At the ER, a new set of doctors and nurses began a round of finger sticks and blood draws, ruling out the simple things. The CAT scan, tests, and blood work all came back inconclusive. So they gave me a prescription for migraines, an appointment with a neurologist, and sent me home.

Once I got in to see the neurologist, he scheduled an MRI and then we had to wait for the reading. Days slipped by between appointments as we braced ourselves for the worst. Those seemed to be the longest days; waiting and not knowing. But there would be longer days in my future. I just didn't know it yet. The MRI showed nothing but a healthy brain. I wondered how healthy it really was since I was disappointed instead of relieved by the results. Not knowing was making me crazy. I continued to manifest real symptoms that no one could explain. The neurologist began to treat me for migraines but also referred me to an ear, nose, and throat doctor since I was beginning to lose my hearing in both ears. All sounds were muffled by this time as if my ears were stopped up.

I shuffled around from doctor to doctor, with no explanation for my apparent symptoms. We braced ourselves at each appointment for the proverbial shoe to drop. It never did. I should have been relieved. But I couldn't get away from the fact that something was wrong with me. With each new doctor came a new prescription as they began treating symptoms. There were no signs of a brain tumor. You would think we would have been relieved, but we were not. We just wanted to know what we were dealing with and how to fix it. The not knowing was scaring us to death. We weren't buying into the doctor's diagnosis of migraines and vertigo, so we kept looking. All the while our fear of the unknown was growing.

With a swimmy head and constant dizziness, I physically could not get out of bed. For six weeks, I would remain confined to my home. Being out of the office for any length of time was challenging. With employees and clients, there was always someone needing something. Being the owner of my business for over 15 years, I knew the importance of being in the office. I had no idea what six weeks would do to my business. It didn't matter, because I simply could not do it. I could not make myself go into the office. I could not even get out of bed.

My body had shut down. The voice on the other end of the phone was too much for my mind to bear. It hurt my ears, head, and brain. Emails or texts on the screen of my cellphone squiggled, making them unreadable. I'm not sure if my eyes were fluttering or my hands were shaking, but it felt like my brain was trembling inside my skull. I could feel it quivering. I was petrified. I could not stand the sound of music, no matter how soft. The noise from the television sent me into a frenzy. Conversation with me was impossible. I could not even handle listening to my husband and son talking in the other room. My brain wanted to listen, but, instead, it muffled and jumbled the sounds. I could not process the words coming out of their mouths and was unable to form sentences in response. Yes and no questions were all I could muster, and, often, these seemed too much. I just wanted silence. But even the quiet seemed too much to endure.

One really bad day, I climbed into bed, pulling the covers up over my head to block the light that was coming in through the window. The weight of my comforter across my body made me feel safe. The rise and fall of the bedding synchronized with my breath, causing the fabric to rustle against my ear, sending me into a frenzy. I was in sensory overload. Forced to disconnect from my friends, family, my business, and the world, I inadvertently disconnected from God. I could not communicate what was happening to me, but I believed God had already left me at the onslaught of this medical crisis. I laid in my bed, under my covers, for seven straight days and nights. That was all I could do. But it didn't matter, because laying there didn't make it better. It didn't make it go away. It didn't change anything. I couldn't get away from whatever it was, whatever I was going through. When I could process thoughts, I knew enough to be terrified that my brain had somehow broken and that my fate was to be lived out lying in this bed for the rest of my days.

My friends and family wanted to help. But, seriously, what could they do? My mom would come and do laundry and put away the dishes. She would try to comfort me by talking with me. Pretending to be asleep, I would pull the blanket up over my head when she arrived. She wanted me to reassure her that her little girl was going to be okay, but I couldn't. It was easier to hide. Talking hurt my head, and I had no answers anyway. It was a hard place to be.

As loving individuals, we want to help. Often, when situations linger, we don't know what to do. I had one friend who came and sat in the dark with me. I laid on the couch under my blanket, blinds drawn, lights off, TV off. I just laid there in the dark—in the silence. She sat in the chair next to me. She didn't talk or ask me questions. She just sat with me. I guess it was comforting at the time. Nothing really mattered then. I was hunkered down, waiting out my personal storm. Looking back, her just being with me was one of the most loving acts of kindness anyone has ever done for me.

Henri Nouwen says, "Be careful when life's questions swirl around you in times of pain. Beware of easy answers or guarantees. Seek the companionship of others who will befriend you and listen as you live the questions of your life. Living into a new way of self-understanding and spiritual depth is aided by having a sturdy spiritual companion or soul friend. The best guide is willing to be silent yet present, and are comfortable with knowing God's Spirit is ultimately the sole source of spiritual guidance, comfort, and knowing."[10] Everyone needs a soul friend, someone willing to sit with you in your darkest hour, to be with you in your silence. Not someone to comfort you or do things for you, someone willing to be with you. In another's time of need, our presence is the greatest gift we can offer.

During this time, I could not pray. I could not even think. I was just there, shriveled up in a heap of flesh. Lying in my bed, clinging to the little bit of self I had left, was the most vulnerable place I had ever been. The fragility of life was upon me. Unbeknownst to me, God was at work. Even when you think God is not there, God is there. God is always working on our behalf. Even when you can't see, hear, or feel God, rest assured, God is at work. What is faith anyway?

The Bible says, "Faith is being sure of what we hope for and certain of what we do not see[11]." I certainly could not see anything, most of all God. All those years of practicing my faith, saying what I believed, serving, and doing as called fell short in those hours. How quickly I forgot everything I knew to be true. As I look back on this time, I thought God had forgotten me. But what surprised me more was how quickly I forgot my own practice. God was there, though, right in the middle of it all.

In my toughest times, God is there, whether we realize it or not. In those moments, God reveals who He is and who He is in us. Often, it takes

---

[10] Henri Nouwen, Spiritual Direction, Wisdom for the Long Walk of Faith, 7–8.
[11] Hebrews 11:1 New International Version (NIV).

looking back to see it. It is important to remember God loves us and wants the very best for us. God "will never leave you nor forsake you[12]." And even though I didn't realize it, God was working things out for me. Issues I didn't even know needed to be worked out were being worked on by God. God goes before us.

This all led me to some pretty important questions. Questions that I was already asking myself before my medical crisis. Questions I would like to ask you. As I am looking back at one of the most difficult times in my life, I would encourage you to look back over your life. We live in the present, but we learn from the past. Pete Scazzero says in his book, *Emotionally Healthy Spirituality*, "True spirituality frees us to live joyfully in the present. It requires, however, going back in order to go forward. This takes us to the very heart of spirituality and discipleship in the family of God—breaking free from the destructive sinful patterns of our pasts to live the life of love God intends.[13]" I want to live the life of love God intends for me. Pete says repeatedly in his book that we must go back in order to go forward.

During my medical crisis, there was nothing anyone could have told me that would have helped me or made me feel better. When you are in it, you are in it. Just know this: God is in it, too. He's right there with you even if you can't feel Him. I believe there is wisdom that can be gleaned from this book. I would encourage you to move at your own pace.

I remember one day my sister called me to see how I was doing. She told me that she believed what was happening to me was spiritual. I was so angry with her. How dare she even suggest such a thing. But from the outside looking in, she had a better vantage point. She knew it was spiritual. She knew it was God. I could not see it, nor did I want to hear

---

[12] Hebrews 13:5 NIV.
[13] Pete Scazzero, Emotionally Healthy Spirituality, 93.

it. What she said was true. However, just because you can see it, doesn't mean you need to say it. Prayer would have probably been a better alternative to telling me what she thought, as I wasn't ready to hear it.

We want to help. We want to fix. We want to make it all better. Often, we want to do because it makes us feel better, as if we've helped in some way. It elevates our self. This is one of the lessons I had to learn. I've done the very same thing my sister did. What she said was out of love and truth. But truth often hurts. So, when speaking truth, first assess the situation. Is the person ready to hear the truth? Can you speak the truth in love? How might your words be received? Prayer is the best step forward. Even before speaking or sharing, pause and breathe into the moment and let the Holy Spirit guide you.

Think back to one of the most difficult times in your life. What were some of the lessons you learned? In hindsight, can you see the good that came out of it? Can you see God now when maybe you could not before? Did God work something out for you? Do you have a new and deeper understanding of God? I would encourage you to reflect on these questions. This is when things get interesting. When I say "things," I mean transformation, growth, realizations about who you are and who you are to God. Grab your journal, notebook, or a piece of scrap paper. Write down the answers to these questions. Let's work through this together. One last thing, these lessons—the look-backs—are opportunities to teach and equip us. I hope the next time I find myself curled up in a heap of flesh under my covers, I remember that even though I could not see God back then, God was there. Just like God is here now. My prayer is that I remember. My lesson is God is always with me. And God is with you, too.

MELISSA H. THOMPSON

I want to ask you the following questions.

1. **Who is God? And who is God to you?** Use the space below to answer this question. There are no wrong answers. No one is looking, just you. The more you give, the more you will receive. The space below will not be enough room. (Just below this exercise is a section entitled **Jumpstart**. It is an alternate exercise designed to do just what it says, jumpstart you and get your thoughts rolling. Use it if you like, but you don't have to. It's only there to help aid you in this journey. Below the **Jumpstart** is a section entitled, "**Just the Facts.**" This is scripture's response to the question. I hope you will find this helpful and comforting as we dig in and move through this together.

Jumpstart:

Close your eyes and take a deep breath in through your nose. Hold it for a two-count and release it out through your mouth, slowly and controlled. With your eyes closed, think of God. Who is God? Who is God to you? What do you see? How do you envision God? See God? Spend some time here. Do not rush. Breathe into this exercise. When you are ready, open your eyes and write down what you saw, felt, or experienced. Jot down any words that pop into your head. Remember, there are no wrong answers. For me, I see bright, white light. I feel warmth and comfort. I feel love.

God is right there in front of me, waiting for me to talk to Him. He is close. He looks at me in great detail with a smile, understanding + fully knowing me + yet loves me all the same.

In this exercise, God reminded me of experiences I have with Beneiah as we are face-to-face talking. I am in the moment with him + yet it is the same time

Standing still, looking, really looking at him, understanding & knowing him in as much detail as I possibly can.

THE ME DISEASE

Just the Facts:

- **Exodus 3:14 NIV;** "I AM WHO I AM."

- **Revelation 22:13 ESV;** "I am the Alpha and the Omega, the first and the last, the beginning and the end."

- **Deuteronomy 6:4 KJV;** "The Lord our God is one Lord"

- **1 John 4:16 TLB;** "We know how much God loves us because we have felt his love and because we believe him when he tells us that he loves us dearly. God is love, and anyone who lives in love is living with God and God is living in him."

- **1 Corinthians 14:33 CEB;** "God isn't a God of disorder but of peace."

- **1 John 1:5 NIV;** "God is light, in him there is no darkness at all."

2. **Do you experience God in your life? Have you experienced the presence of God or the Holy Spirit? Where have you seen God at work today?** As you write, highlight or underline words that pop out at you. Notice how you feel as you answer these questions. Reflect on **Just the Facts**. What words jump out at you in **reference** to God. Journal your thoughts.

Jumpstart:

Often I feel God's presence when I sing a song or when I'm listening to music. The words seem to penetrate my soul and unlock some mysterious place deep within. Sometimes I feel God in nature, the warm breeze on my face, or the sound of birds chirping back and forth to one another. I have experienced God through acts of kindness, like when I see a child holding the door for an elderly person, and I'm overwhelmed by emotion. One of my favorite places to experience God is in the trees, the bigger the better. There's something about the leaves rustling around as the limbs sway back and forth. I love the enormity of the tree trunk, with its roots burrowing down deep into the earth. I sense God in the trees.

Just the Facts: God's Presence

- **Exodus 33:14 NIV;** My Presence will go with you, and I will give you rest."

- **Jeremiah 29:12-13 NLT;** When you pray, I will listen. If you look for me wholeheartedly, you will find me.

- **Matthew 18:20 ESV;** For where two or three are gathered in my name, there am I among them.

- **Psalm 34:8 CEB;** Taste and see how good the Lord is! The one who takes refuge in him is truly happy!

3. **Think about one of the hardest times in your life. Can you see God there now in retrospect? Did you realize it at the time? What are the things that brought you the most comfort?** Journal your thoughts about that time in your life. List all acts of kindness, regardless of how small. Be sure to come back and review your answers once you reach the end of the book to see how your ideas and thoughts have transformed.

Jumpstart:

When I was sick, I thought God had left me. Looking back, I see that God was with me through the birds chirping outside my window, the warmth of the sun on my face, friends who sat with me, a sister that called to check on me daily, church family that sent me cards, a mother who would come and do my laundry, and a husband and son who tended to my every need. God was everywhere. Looking back now, can you see that God was with you even though you thought you were alone?

Just the Facts: God in the Darkest Days

- **Psalm 20:1 NIV;** May the LORD answer you when you are in distress; may the name of the God of Jacob protect you. May he send you help from the sanctuary and grant you support from Zion.

- **Psalm 9:9 CEB;** The Lord is a safe place for the oppressed—a safe place in difficult times.

- **Psalm 86:7 The Message;** Every time I'm in trouble I call on you, confident that you'll answer.

- **John 14:1 AMP;** Do not let your heart be troubled (afraid, cowardly). Believe [confidently] in God and trust in Him, [have faith, hold on to it, rely on it, keep going and] believe also in Me.

I've included a prayer for you at the end of each chapter. Pray the prayer for yourself. Take your time as you move through each chapter, the questions, the scriptures, and the prayer. I often find comfort in praying the scriptures. You may want to do that. Be mindful of your breath as you move through the questions, scriptures, and prayer. Breathe in through your nose for a count of three, hold it, and release through your mouth ever so slowly. Do this at least two or three times before you begin the prayer. This will help to settle your spirit and center your mind. I frequently experience God through breathing exercises. Use this technique as often as you need to.

Prayer: Dear Lord, I want to know you more. Show me who you are and who you are to me. Help me to see you at work in all things. If I cannot see you, build my faith, so that I am confident that YOU are still with me. Thank you for your Word that reminds me that in my day of trouble, I will call on you and you will answer me. That I can seek you and find you. That you are my Beginning and my End, my Light and my Love. Continue to guide me on my path and help me to be all that you have created me to be. In Jesus' name, Amen.

Chapter Two

Little Signs

JUST BEFORE MY MEDICAL CRISIS, I had been doing a lot of soul-searching. At the time, I was my pastor's lay leader of the church I had attended my entire life. Being the lay leader meant I was the liaison between the congregation and the pastor. This role came with a lot of responsibility and required a great deal of my time. I didn't mind. I was in love with the church. Because of my role, I attended every church meeting. All of them! And there were a lot. I helped with small group studies, Wednesday night fellowship meals, and local mission work. I even led the worship service from time to time and delivered a message when needed. I sang in the choir and with the praise team.

We were a small church, so there was plenty of work to be done. It makes me think of the scripture, "The harvest is plentiful, but the workers are few.[14]" I carried this misunderstanding of the scripture around with me to justify my growing resentment. I was a worker and proud of all the work I did for the church. I was also proud of the position and proud of my dedication to the church. I had been a part of

---

[14] Matthew 9:35, I would encourage you to read the whole text. Scripture should always be read in context, understanding place, time and audience.

this congregation since birth. Actually, my mom was attending while pregnant, so really before birth. I was proud of that fact, too. Both my parents and grandparents attended church there. In fact, my grandfather helped build the old church and then helped build the new one. With the birth of my son, we were a four-generational family. I was sitting "high in my seat," if you know what I mean. I had longevity, history, and you know the old saying, "Knowledge is power." Lots of signs of unhealthy behavior were beginning to seep out of me: pride, resentment, power, control. If you had pointed them out to me, I would have been offended. You would not have known it, though, unless you picked up on my passive-aggressive response of "Well, there's plenty of work to do, just not enough people to do it." If you didn't catch the hint, I might just offer to pray with you, pray that you would start working as hard I was. Praying always seemed to be the right thing to do to deflect a situation.

Just prior to my breakdown, things began to change for me. I joined a small group at the church and began meeting regularly. Our first study was entitled *Emotionally Healthy Spirituality* by Pete Scazzero[15]. This study caused me to begin asking many questions about what I believed and why I believed it. Through the study, we were asked to trace our family tree. We were looking for behaviors exhibited in our parents that might have been passed down to us. My excitement rose as I began to understand that my beliefs were based on what I was taught. I learned that my faith had been handed down from my grandfather to my mother. She modified it for herself and then handed it to me. Imagine my surprise when I discovered that I had my mother's faith. I also have some of her behaviors. I'm a people pleaser and a conflict avoider. By the end of the

---

[15] https://www.emotionallyhealthy.org/ this is a countercultural discipleship study designed to move people from shallow Christianity to depth in Christ. This study was instrumental in my discipleship journey.

study, I knew more about why I did the things I did and where they came from. At least one generation's characteristics anyway.

Out of this study, my inquisitiveness grew. I began questioning everything: why I believed what I believed, why I did certain things, and why I reacted the way I did. Tracing other people's behaviors became a game to me, almost like connecting the dots with light bulb moments of understanding behaviors exhibited in others. Looking at myself was a little harder. But I was uncovering so much new information. Things about myself, my family, my church, and my faith. I just didn't realize what all that uncovering was actually doing to me on the inside. When you uncover something, like an old wound, you either have to treat it or cover it back up. I was uncovering a lot of old wounds.

My husband, Travis, was the first to notice something was happening to me during this study. He is what we "churchgoers" would call a "pew warmer." He would come to church with me on Sunday morning but would not join in any study. He was comfortable being a pew warmer. But it upset me. There was just so much work to do. We needed all able bodies to get the job done, whatever the job was at the time. And at the church, there was always a job to do: a fundraiser, a dinner to serve, things to clean, rooms to set up, people to minister to. My resentment was growing. I found myself thinking, if I was going to work this hard for the church, he should, too. Travis did not feel the same way.

Often, he would remind me how hard I was working for the church. This was a source of contention between us. Our arguing increased, as my time spent at the church did too. He did what he wanted to do, which was church on Sunday mornings only. I did what I wanted to, which was to be there every time the doors were opened. It seemed the doors were open all the time. I began to feel like it was expected of me to be there. I think I expected it of myself. I was there a lot, and he was not. He continued trying to discuss it. But I was not willing to admit there was a problem or even talk about it. Compromising was out of the question. He wasn't willing to do any more, and I wasn't willing to do any less. I was working for God. And I told him so, often. Frustrated, I would think, "How dare he ask me to choose him over God?" I justified myself because, well, it was God. But I didn't know the difference between God and church and had somehow confused the two.

My unhealthy behaviors continued to grow. At the very least, my work ethic with the church helped me maintain a sense of power and control. Either way, it was beginning to feel icky. Church should not feel icky. Church should be a safe place where you can come and just be and learn to grow as a disciple of Jesus Christ. Despite the ugly feelings I was having, I loved my church. The signs of disease continued to show in me and on me. False expectations, assuming outcomes, possessiveness, more signs that the inside of me was going awry.

One weekend, we decided to get out of town and go to the lake. The lake has always been my happy place, and it always gave Travis and me a chance to reconnect. In the laziness of the day, we often discussed our hopes and dreams, our beliefs, and thoughts on God or a certain scripture. On this weekend, I was questioning God, my faith, and why I believed what I believed. We were going around and around. I could tell Travis was getting nervous. At one point, Travis stopped me in mid-sentence and blurted out, "I have always stood on your faith. If your faith falls apart where does that leave me?" I looked him squarely in the eyes and said, "You can't stand on someone else's faith. You have to stand on your own." No sooner than the words left my mouth, I felt sick in the pit of my stomach, as a wave of truth covered me: I had done the same thing with my mother's faith. I was standing on hers; he was standing on mine. No wonder I felt like I was about to collapse. I wasn't sure what I believed anymore. However, I did know why I believed it. Because my mama told me so.

This was hard stuff to unpack. Things just weren't adding up anymore. The easy answers didn't cut it. I knew something was off with me and my faith. I just didn't know how to fix it. Everything was all jumbled up. I didn't know what to do, so I just kept doing what I had been doing: asking questions. Travis knew I was heading for trouble. Later that same day, he admitted that I had always been the rock of our household. He was scared, and I was tired of arguing. Instead of reassuring him that everything was going to be okay, I quickly retorted, "Well, there just might come a time when I can't be the rock anymore. What are you going to do then? You might have to stand up and be the rock." We didn't know it at the time, but God was foreshadowing our future for us. This conversation was prophetic. Down deep inside, I knew something was coming. Travis knew, too. He could see it. My faith was shaking, and so was I. This was four weeks prior to my breakdown. Travis had no choice but to be the rock for our family. He's a natural at it, too. This is one of the many things God righted for us out of my medical crisis. God is always working it out for the good of those who love Him.[16]

A few days after we returned from the lake, I was driving to my mom's house, and I had this vision. I could see myself standing before a huge Jenga[17] set. In the game, wooden blocks are stacked three by three in a tower. Each player takes a turn removing a block one by one until the foundation is compromised, and the tower of blocks falls to the ground. Whoever pulls the block that causes the tower to fall loses the game. In the vision, I could see the stack of Jenga blocks. Except these blocks were enormous, like giant Jenga, at least five times taller than I am. I

---

[16] Romans 8:28 NIV

[17] Jenga is a game of physical skill created by Leslie Scott, and currently marketed by Hasbro. Players take turns removing one block at a time from a tower constructed of 54 blocks. Each block removed is then placed on top of the tower, creating a progressively taller and more unstable structure.

stood at the base of the structure, looking up at the stack of wooden blocks, my neck craned back to see the top.

Illustration by Grace Gainey

I watched the gigantic tower sway back and forth, anticipating its fall. Intuitively, I knew a couple of things. One, the tower represented my faith. Two, it was about to come crashing down. Before it fell, I noticed each block had a word on it. As is collapsed before me, I stood there in amazement at the heap of debris. Immediately, I began working. With my own hands, I worked to rebuild the structure block by block. But instead of building it straight up three by three, as it was before, I placed the blocks long ways, still three high. I began reading the words on each block.

I kept working until all the pieces had been used. These were the same blocks with the same words. I used every piece. I had no idea who built the first tower, but, with my own hands, I laid the foundation of this one.

Illustration by Grace Gainey

When I placed the last block, I climbed up on this new foundation, laid down, and rested upon it. This was my new faith. It was complete.

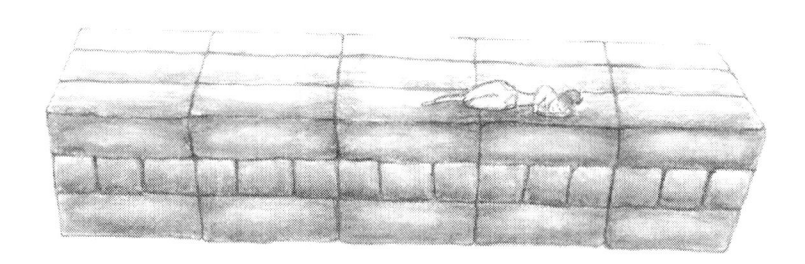

Illustration by Grace Gainey

THE ME DISEASE

As I pulled into my mom's driveway, I came out of the vision, mesmerized by I what I had just seen. I threw the car in park, grabbed a scrap piece of paper and pen, and began jotting down all the details of this incredible experience. All this did was lead me to more questions.

---

1. **What do I believe?** Regarding my faith and God, what do I believe? Use the space below to begin writing down what you believe.

Jumpstart:

I believe in God the Father Almighty. I also believe in Jesus as God's son and I believe in the Holy Spirit. I was taught to believe in the Trinity, but I cannot quite get my mind around the three in one that Christians often speak of. That's okay. You can take all your questions to God. God can handle it. I also believe that God is love. I believe that we love because God first loved us[18]. I believe that God is our creator, and that God created all things. I do not understand how God could have possibly created everything in seven days, but I don't have to understand creation. I do get to participate in creation.

Just the Facts:

- **1 Corinthians 8:6 NIV;** yet for us there is but one God, the Father, from whom all things came and for whom we live; and there is but one Lord, Jesus Christ, through whom all things came and through whom we live.

---

[18] 1 John 4:10 NIV

- **Romans 11:33-34 The Message;** Is there anyone around who can explain God? Anyone smart enough to tell him what to do? Anyone who has done him such a huge favor that God has to ask his advice?
  Everything comes from him;
  Everything happens through him;
  Everything ends up in him.

- **1 John 4:10 NLT;** This is real love—not that we loved God, but that he loved us and sent his Son as a sacrifice to take away our sins.

- I would encourage you to find your own scriptures to support what you believe. Google it. List them here. Then look those scriptures up, read them and read around them, meaning what comes before and after them.

2. **Do you know why you believe what you believe? Was it taught to you?** Handed down from generation to generation from grandmother to mother to you? Did you learn it on your own through research and experience? Did you learn it through Sunday School or Vacation Bible School that you attended as a child? Does your knowledge come from the Bible or a person? There are no wrong answers.

Jumpstart:

Why do you believe what you believe? Do you know? I have been in church all my life. I never thought to ask why I believe what I believe. The more I questioned, the more questions I came up with. Don't be afraid. I say this because I was scared to death—afraid, I guess, that I might find out that it was all a hoax, like some big made-up story to make us all feel better about life. Whatever you are feeling, it's okay. We can take all our questions and all our fears to God. God can handle it.

Just the Facts:

- **2 Timothy 3:16 NIV;** All Scripture is God-breathed and is useful for teaching, rebuking, correcting, and training in righteousness.

- **John 14:6 NLT;** Jesus told him, "I am the way, the truth, and the life. No one can come to the Father except through me."

- **John 6:29 KJV;** Jesus answered and said unto them, "This is the work of God, that ye believe on him whom he hath sent."

- **John 4:42 NIV;** We no longer believe just because of what you said; now we have heard for ourselves, and we know that this man really is the Savior of the world.

3. **What are the feelings you have when you think about church, the Bible, God, Jesus, the Holy Spirit? What do your parents or grandparents think about church, the Bible, God, Jesus, the Holy Spirit? Could you have a conversation with them about why they believe what they believe?**

Jumpstart:

When you think about church, what images or feelings immediately come into your mind? Write those down. Now think about your parents or even your grandparents, what were their thoughts or feelings about church? Are the thoughts or feelings similar? Are they opposite? Notice your feelings as you move through this exercise. Apply to each one, church, the Bible, God, Jesus, the Holy Spirit. Why do you feel the way you feel? Were you taught to feel this way? How do you really feel?

Just the Facts: The Church:

- **Matthew 16:18 CEB;** I tell you that you are Peter. And I'll build my church on this rock. The gates of the underworld won't be able to stand against it.

- **Hebrews 10:24-25 NIV;** let us consider how we may spur one another on toward love and good deeds, not giving up meeting together, as some are in the habit of doing, but encouraging one another . . .

The Bible:

- **John 1:1 NLT;** In the beginning the Word already existed. The Word was with God, and the Word was God.

- **Hebrews 4:12 CEB;** Because God's word is living, active, and sharper than any two-edged sword, it penetrates to the point that it separates the soul from the spirit and the joints from the marrow. It's able to judge the heart's thoughts and intentions.

God:

- All of scripture speaks of who God is. I covered some scriptures about Who God is and who the Bible says God is in Chapter One. Please refer back to those references, or you can search scripture yourself and create your own list.

Jesus:

- **1 Timothy 2:5 ESV;** For there is one God, and there is one mediator between God and men, the man Christ Jesus.

- **Acts 4:11-12 NIV;** Jesus is 'the stone you builders rejected, which has become the cornerstone.' Salvation is found in no one else, for there is no other name under heaven given to mankind by which we must be saved.

The Holy Spirit:

- **John 14:26 CEB;** The Companion, the Holy Spirit, whom the Father will send in my name, will teach you everything and will remind you of everything I told you.

- **John 14:15-17 NLT;** If you love me, obey my commandments. And I will ask the Father, and he will give you another Advocate, who will never leave you. He is the Holy Spirit, who leads into all truth. The world cannot receive him, because it isn't looking for him and doesn't recognize him. But you know him, because he lives with you now and later will be in you.

Prayer: Dear Lord, thank you that you have given us your Word to teach us who You are, who Jesus is, and who the Holy Spirit is. Continue to show us the way you would have us go. Help us to bring our thoughts, feelings, and emotions about You, Jesus, the Holy Spirit, and Church to You. Teach us to reflect on your truth knowing that we can trust you. In Jesus' name, Amen.

Chapter Three

Where it all Began: The Symptoms

THINKING BACK ON ALL THE things that led up to my breakdown, I realize I was blind to my own circumstances. I had developed unhealthy behaviors, both in my personal life and spiritual life. My growing resentment for both my husband and the church was a new symptom spurred on by the contention between the two. It was obvious my deep-seated control issues had been around for quite some time.

Pete Scazzero teaches, "What happens in one generation often repeats itself in the next. The consequences of actions and decisions taken in one generation affect those who follow. For this reason, it is common to observe certain patterns from one generation to the next such as divorce, alcoholism, addictive behavior, sexual abuse, poor marriages, one child running off, mistrust of authority, pregnancy out of wedlock, an inability to sustain stable relationships, etc.[19]" I believe just as we hand down certain patterns, we hand down our behaviors, our fears, how we handle

---

[19] Pete Scazzero, Emotionally Healthy Spirituality, 95–96.

conflict, and how we relate to one another. Pete states, "True spirituality frees us to live joyfully in the present. It requires, however, going back in order to go forward. This takes us to the very heart of spirituality and discipleship in the family of God—breaking free from the destructive sinful patterns of our pasts to live the life of love God intends."[20] We really must go back before we can go forward. Looking back, tracing my own generational tree set me on a course, as I was trying to understand why I was the way I was. It led me all the way back to my childhood where often our behaviors are molded and shaped before we can even remember.

The year was 1978, and I was five. Back then, kids played outside. The television only came on after the supper dishes were hand washed, dried, and put away. The minutes ticked by like hours from dinner until TV time. Mama cleaned up after the meal, and I watched. Seldom did I help. I wasn't expected to, therefore I didn't. It was a new age, and my mama was doing her thing. She worked a full-time job, tended to her family, and made sure there was a home cooked meal on the table every night that Daddy was home. He was a fireman, which meant he was gone for 24 hours at a time every other day. My mama was a farmer's daughter. They were expected to work.

Now my grandpa—her father; that was a different story. He was one of 11 siblings. They were farmers, too. They were not expected to work, they were born for it. With eleven kids, you didn't have to hire help in the fields. You had your own. My mama's farm days were lighter than her father's. But there was still tobacco in the summer and potatoes in the fall. Farming was hard work. You did what you had to do. Like it or not, everyone pitched in. If my mom resented her days on the farm, she never said so. But now she wasn't on the farm. She was in her own home with

---

[20] Pete Scazzero, Emotionally Healthy Spirituality, 93.

her own family in the city. She loved my sister and me. She cooked, she cleaned, she did it all. We watched. She was made to work, and she wanted better for us.

With my dad being gone every other day, I really don't know how she did it. But we didn't mind when daddy wasn't there because that's when we did all the fun stuff. We would go out to eat at McDonald's for supper, stay up late telling stories, and sleep in the bed with Mama. I always had to be the hamburger, meaning I was in the middle. I guess because I was the youngest. It was the best! I began cultivating a sense of togetherness that I still have today. I love to be together. The closer the better.

On the nights he was home, after suppertime, Daddy would turn the knob on the tube TV and recline back in his easy chair. I sat in anticipation as the old TV would buzz and click, and then, like magic, a fuzzy picture would emerge. I would hop on the arm of the couch nearest him, or climb up between his legs, and recline back on his belly. It was my favorite place. We watched whatever Daddy watched, and we were fine with it.

My TV time was Saturday mornings around 6:30 a.m. Just like my mama, I have always been an early riser. With Bugs Bunny and Elmer Fudd as my early morning hosts, Saturdays have always been the best day ever. After that, I watched *The Super Friends*, "Wonder Twins Power Activate!" I'm pretty sure that's where the fist bump came from. I loved the superheroes and was pretty sure I had some superpowers of my own. I'm not sure when *The Smurfs* came along, but I loved them, too. Being my favorite, I collected all the Smurf branded drinking glasses from the local fast-food restaurant. I always felt sorry for Smurfette, though. Being the only female smurf in Smurf Village seemed strange to me. However, when I myself entered the corporate world and then later owned my own business, I found it to be much the same. It was definitely a man's world, and I was one little Smurfette.

One Saturday afternoon, long after the cartoons were over, I found myself in our backyard. The day had slipped away. We were fortunate to live in a neighborhood filled with kids of all ages. On this day, however, there were none around. It was okay, though. I made my own friends as my imagination crafted and created whatever I wanted.

With the crisp, cool wind brushing through the reddish leaves, I stood on the back of our concrete stoop alone. That stoop was my stage. I was the conductor of a brilliant choir. The members were the trees with their arms of thin limbs morphing out with skinny hands and long spindly fingers. Vibrantly, this imaginary choir, which happened to be pines, swayed back and forth, reaching high into the Carolina blue sky. Their movement was contagious as my body synchronized with them. My arms flowed along, dancing with their movement. The most magical part was the unseen force collaborating with my efforts to create this beautiful musical. I couldn't see it or hear it. But, I could feel it. Light and crisp at times, whipping upward in a whoosh of an unseen force that would tickle my hair along my face. Challenging my majestic choir higher and higher, we danced and moved together.

We were a trio: me, the trees, and the wind. In perfect unison, we moved together, each of us believing they were, in fact, the conductor of this symphonic liturgical melody. All the while, knowing that I was really the conductor. Orchestrating this endeavor of musical delight, I knew I was in control of it all. As the wind picked up, so did our dance. With closed eyes, arms lifted high, and hands gliding through the air, I would catch hold of the force, and push it left and then right. The wind obeyed my every command, just as the trees did. As my arms raised higher, the wind grew bolder, and the trees bent further. The music was building in my mind, causing the movements to become fearless. In a growing crescendo, we were heading toward a climactic finish. And right at that pivotal moment, just before the grand finale, I hear, "Melllliiiiisssssaaaa . . ." from my mother just behind me. "Time for dinner!" she yelled. The screen door slammed before I could even turn around. The whole cantata fell flat. My arms dropped, the trees stopped swaying, and the wind ran and hid. Just like that, it was over. I rolled my eyes in disgust and headed inside for dinner. However, I knew, in that moment, I had found my superpower. I could control the wind. How many people could do that? And I believed it, too.

Even at age five, I was beginning to understand my superiority and the great power that lay within me. I was already cultivating an amazing ability to control things. And I liked it. Years later, I would hone this skill to a whole new level, known only to me as "The Super Freak." My powers were increasing. Control freak was for the average, but there is nothing average about me. And my ability to control . . . everything. Think about it, really. Who thinks they can control the wind? I know I was only five, and kids have active imaginations, but, as I grew up, I traded the wind for a new toy, a bigger force similar in nature. The Holy Spirit. Just as I thought I was controlling the wind, I thought I could control the Spirit. As I grew, I realized that in obeying the Spirit, the Spirit would continue to speak. Ultimately, there is no greater challenge than one who can control . . . God. Through the Spirit, I had this direct connection. And like most things, I was proud of it.

I believed that, if I thanked God enough, HE would give me everything I wanted. I would twist my prayers into some kind of "genie in a bottle"; God not only supplying my every need but also my every want. Do you know what happens to a child that gets everything he or she wants? Let me just say, "spoiled-rotten brat." Add on a layer of "holier than thou" spirituality, and you have a recipe for disaster. More like a sickness, or, as I like to call it, *the Me Disease.* It's the kind of disease that lies unnoticed under the skin, growing while no one notices. It's that sneaky

THE ME DISEASE

kind of disease that creeps into every area of your life and takes over before you even know you have it. The kind that affects your family and relationships.

The symptoms vary. You don't have to be like me—a control freak, power hungry, and prideful. But you might be. I see it in a lot of people. It's running rampant, and no one seems to notice. In fact, in our society, we encourage it and even promote it. Competition is prevalent. Be the best! I'm number one! Got to get to the top! This is the life that we live. At least, some of us. It's socially acceptable to be proud of yourself, your family, your kids, your job, your success, your accomplishments, your bank account, your big house, or big car. It's all about me, what I have, and what I am doing. It is easy to fall into this trap.

Maybe you think I'm being overly dramatic. But I can trace the steps that led me to my breakdown. I can see how I shifted in my thinking and twisted situations and conversations to make them more about me and less about the other person, often under the guise of God. I see what happened and how I got off course. But I do realize it is in our failures and mistakes that we learn our greatest lessons. Seldom do we learn anything from our wins. Our successes set us up for failure. But our failures build us up for life. They make us grow, stretch, and turn into the people we were created to be. Failure is our way back home.

Even today, I am still recovering from what I call *the Me Disease*. Maybe I always will be, like a recovering addict. This disease has so many symptoms. Control freak just happens to be one of mine, along with pride and the tendency to manipulate. These go hand in hand. Obsessed with my own self, the ego will step on or over anyone in order to grow bigger. This is the fake self that I created for myself, not the true self God created me to be. Right before the breakdown, as I continued to uncover those questions, I kept uncovering parts of myself that had been infected by this disease. I had become a professional at the coverup.

Back when I was five and controlling the wind was probably one of the first signs. "Hello, my name is Melissa Thompson, and I have *the Me Disease.*" I need a weekly meeting to attend.

Those of us aware that we suffer from the Me Disease need some kind of 12-step program to help with our recovery. The likelihood is that I have inflicted this disease on others, unaware of the damage I am doing to myself and them. But, that's what it does. You don't really care what you are doing to others. It's all about me. Looking back a little further, I remember my mother wanting to instill confidence in her adorably pudgy, pig-tailed daughter. She would sing "Here she comes, Miss America," as I entered the kitchen every morning for breakfast. And I get it. Today, I build my son up with words, convincing him of his greatness. Doesn't every mother want their child to feel like they are the center of the universe? I'll never forget listening to Beth Moore speak at a women's conference. She said, and I'm paraphrasing, "If your child acts like he's the king of your house, who do you think put that crown on his head? It might be time to remove the crown." We make our children into kings and queens. And then we get mad at them when they start acting like it. They think the world revolves around them because we have treated them as if it does. What are they going to do when they go out on their own and realize that the world does not revolve around them?

We have an obligation to ourselves and to our children to begin straightening out some of our generational junk. It is a scary thought. I hope and pray my child gets the best of me. Unfortunately, we don't get to choose. They get it all. My mom singing the Miss America song was a simple act of love that had a profound impact on who I was becoming. I was somebody! And not just somebody, I was somebody important! She believed I was as beautiful as any "Miss America." If I traced my mother's tree, I would guess that she wasn't told how beautiful she was as a child. See how it works. We are affected by the previous generation, and we are affecting the next one. My mama loves me so much. I could only hope to be half as beautiful of a person as she is.

As parents, we must be aware of what we are teaching our children. If we aren't careful, we begin believing *who* we think we are, and we forget *whose* we are. Our identity must be rooted in being a beloved child of God. I am a child of God. You are a child of God. It really levels the playing field if we will remember that we are all children from the same God. You are no more important than I am, and I am no more important than you. I am important in the eyes of God, and you are important in the eyes of God. I am loved just as much by God as you are loved by God. Henri Nouwen writes, "First of all, you have to keep unmasking the world about you for what it is: manipulative, controlling, power-hungry, and, in the long run, destructive. The world tells you many lies about who you are, and you simply have to be realistic enough to remind yourself of this. Every time you feel hurt, offended, or rejected, you have to dare to say to yourself: 'These feelings, strong as they may be, are not telling me the truth about myself. The truth, even though I cannot feel it right now, is that I am the chosen child of God, precious in God's eyes, called the Beloved from all eternity, and held safe in an everlasting belief.[21]" It's time to begin looking at ourselves in order to remember the truth of who we are: beloved children of God.

Ask yourself this:

1. **What are some behaviors in other people that irritate you? List them here.**

---

[21] Henri J.M. Nouwen, Life of the Beloved: Spiritual Living in a Secular World

Jumpstart:

Think about the one person that aggravates you the most. This might be a co-worker, a friend, the cashier at the grocery store, or your spouse. Think about the things that frustrate you with this person. Be as specific as you can.

Just the Facts:

- **1 Corinthians 13, The Message;** Love never gives up.
  Love cares more for others than for self.
  Love doesn't want what it doesn't have.
  Love doesn't strut,
  Doesn't have a swelled head,
  Doesn't force itself on others,
  Isn't always "Me first,"
  Doesn't fly off the handle,
  Doesn't keep score of the sins of others,
  Doesn't revel when others grovel,
  Takes pleasure in the flowering of truth,
  Puts up with anything,
  Trusts God always,
  Always looks for the best,
  Never looks back,
  But keeps going to the end.
  Love never dies.

- **Galatians 5:22-26 NIV;** The fruit of the Spirit is love, joy, peace, forbearance, kindness, goodness, faithfulness, gentleness and self-control. Against such things there is no law. Those who belong to Christ Jesus have crucified the flesh with its passions and desires. Since we live by the Spirit, let us keep in step with

THE ME DISEASE

the Spirit. Let us not become conceited, provoking and envying each other.

2. What are some of your own behaviors that frustrate you?

Jumpstart:

Think about a time when you responded poorly to a situation or responded in a way that surprised you. What were the circumstances? Was there a lot of stress or chaos? Think about what led up to that moment. Be honest with yourself, knowing that we often lie to ourselves in an attempt to justify our own behaviors.

Just the Facts:

- **Proverbs 15:1 NLT;** A gentle answer deflects anger, but harsh words make tempers flare.

- **Proverbs 13:10 KJV;** Only by pride cometh contention: but with the well advised is wisdom.

- **Romans 9:25 ESV;** "Those who were not my people I will call 'my people,' and her who was not beloved I will call 'beloved[22]."

---

[22] Beloved; https://www.biblestudytools.com/dictionary/beloved/
A term of affectionate endearment common to both Testaments. Limited chiefly to two Hebrew words and their derivatives: 'ahebh, "to breathe" or "long for," hence, to love, corresponding to the New Testament, agapao, "to prefer," i.e. a love based on respect and benevolent regard; dodh, "love," chiefly love between the sexes, based on sense and emotion, akin to phileo (Latin amare). Both words used of God's love for His chosen:

3. **Do you see any similarities between the behaviors in those that aggravate you and behaviors in yourself that bother you? Take a moment and ponder[23] this question. Then journal your thoughts here.**

Jumpstart:

"We can only see things within others that we see within ourselves. Everyone you meet is your mirror. Why is that? We come to understand ourselves best through our relationships with other people. We can only be triggered by something we have experienced ourselves. The traits we tend to dislike in others are usually the traits we do not like about ourselves. We then tend to judge and criticize these characteristics. This calls to mind the analogy of pointing a blaming finger at someone. One finger is pointing at another person, and three are pointing back to ourselves."[24]

---

e.g. Solomon, "beloved of his God" (Nehemiah 13:26); Benjamin "beloved of Yahweh" (Deuteronomy 33:12); so even of wayward Israel (Jeremiah 11:15).
In the New Testament "beloved" used exclusively of Divine and Christian love, an affection begotten in the community of the new spiritual life in Christ, e.g. "beloved in the Lord" (Romans 16:8). The beauty, unity, endearment of this love is historically unique, being peculiarly Christian.

[23] Merriam-Webster's definition of ponder is this, "to think or consider especially quietly, soberly, and deeply"

[24] http://www.thepowerofoneness.com/blog/what-we-see-in-others-is-a-reflection-of-ourselves/ by Sandra Brossman 2013, Conversely, the behaviors you see in others that you love are a reflection of those same behaviors in yourself.

THE ME DISEASE

Just the Facts:

- **Galatians 3:26-27, The Message;** But now you have arrived at your destination: By faith in Christ you are in direct relationship with God. Your baptism in Christ was not just washing you up for a fresh start. It also involved dressing you in an adult faith wardrobe—Christ's life, the fulfillment of God's original promise.

- **2 Timothy 1:2-7, NIV;** To Timothy, my dear son: Grace, mercy and peace from God the Father and Christ Jesus our Lord.

  I thank God, whom I serve, as my ancestors did, with a clear conscience, as night and day I constantly remember you in my prayers. Recalling your tears, I long to see you, so that I may be filled with joy. I am reminded of your sincere faith, which first lived in your grandmother Lois and in your mother Eunice and, I am persuaded, now lives in you also.

  For this reason, I remind you to fan into flame the gift of God, which is in you through the laying on of my hands. For the Spirit God gave us does not make us timid, but gives us power, love and self-discipline.[25]

- **1 Corinthians 3:21-23, CEB;** So then, no one should brag about human beings. Everything belongs to you—Paul, Apollos, Cephas, the world, life, death, things in the present, things in the future—everything belongs to you, but you belong to Christ, and Christ belongs to God.

---

[25] This is a wonderful scripture example of one generation passing down their faith in God to the next. From Timothy's grandmother to Timothy.

Prayer: Dear Lord, help me to look at others with love even when they are hard to love. Help me to recognize those dark places in myself. Give me the courage to bring all of me to You. Help me to look at myself and others with truth and respond in love. In Jesus' name, Amen.

Chapter Four

The Uncovering
The Shift from Big ME to Little Me

LEADING UP TO THE BREAKDOWN, there was an uncovering that was happening inside me. I'm not certain who was doing the uncovering—me or God. It makes no difference, because it needed to occur. Like pruning. It makes me think of that quote "Once you've seen it, you cannot un-see it."[26] God allowed me to glimpse into myself, and what I saw was ugly. My unhealthy behavior could not be ignored any longer. Once I realized my dysfunction, I had to do something about it. Even if I decided to do nothing at all, I was still doing something. However, I am not one to sit around and twiddle my thumbs. Now, the power, control, and pride were accompanied by a new friend: resentment. Confused by this growing resentment, I realized it was directed toward my husband and the church. My two loves. How quickly

---

[26] Arundhati Roy is an Indian writer who is also an activist who focuses on issues related to social justice and economic inequality. She won the Booker Prize in 1997 for her novel, *The God of Small Things*, and has also written two screenplays and several collections of essays.

my adoration slipped into contempt. They say there's a thin line between love and hate, and suddenly, I found myself on the other side of that line.

I was doing so much service work back then. One time, my small group from church headed for downtown with a cooler full of milk, juice, yogurt, pastries, and cereal. We arrived at a pretty little park and set up our breakfast on a nearby picnic table. The area was known for homeless traffic, and we were hoping to meet a few of the locals. When Albert first approached us, the first thing I noticed was his pants. He grasped them in a bunch with his hand to hold them up. They must have been four sizes too big. We invited him to sit at our table and have breakfast with us. One of my friends ran to her car and emerged with a rope. It was the closest thing we had to a belt. But it worked, and Albert was grateful.

He asked if he could let his cereal soak in the bowl of milk for a while to soften it since he was missing many of his front teeth. This gave us a chance to talk. And it wasn't long before Albert had us mesmerized with his adventures of living on the streets. He had been homeless for over five years. Yet, he had family in the same city. A strange sadness crept in on me as he explained why his family would not have anything to do with him.

He described his days, often having to hide his belongings in hopes they would still be there when he returned later. Sometimes they were, and sometimes they weren't. It made me realize how much I take for granted. I never worry about my personal belongings. I know they are safe in my home. But when you have no home, how do you keep your stuff safe? He could see the concern in my eyes and quickly explained it was best to not have a lot of stuff. Somehow, that thought felt freeing to me.

With pride, he showed us his favorite sleeping spot, which happened to be a park bench. He told us the officers who patrolled the area would generally run him off if they found him there. But some of the cops who knew him would let him stay. We asked him why he didn't stay in the local shelter at night, and he told us a horrifying story of having to fight for a bed. In fact, Albert was asleep in the shelter bed, and some guy jumped on him and began fist-punching him in the head. He explained it was easier and safer to keep to himself out on the streets. As he took his last bite of cereal, he jumped up, thanked us, and headed out of the park. I asked him if he could stay a little longer, but he explained that some construction workers around the corner would let him clean up their work site and give him a few dollars. But he needed to be the first one there to claim the work. We prayed with him before he left. And a tear ran down his face. He said no one ever prayed for him. I asked if I could hug him, and he graciously agreed. There were more tears, but this time they were mine. I told him we would be back and hoped that we would see him again. We did not.

I was in such a hurry loading the car with all the breakfast supplies earlier that morning, I did not have a chance to talk with my husband. Travis would have to take Luke, our son, to school, which was not a big deal. I left the house before they were hardly out of bed. With a kiss on the cheek, I bid them goodbye and reminded Travis of my church meeting after work.

Around 9 p.m., I left the church heading for home. This would not be a big deal if it hadn't become common for me. The closer I got to the house, the more tension I began to feel in my body. I knew I was in trouble with my husband. I began to pray to God that Travis would not be upset or that maybe he would already be asleep. As I quietly entered the house, Travis was sitting in the living room waiting for me. His arms were crossed, and there was a chill in the room. My son was already asleep in his bed. Exhausted, I gave him a pitiful fake smile and braced myself for what came next. There was no faking it on his side. He launched into battle accusing me of having no respect for him or our son. He explained how unfair it was to our family for me to be gone all day and night. I retorted, "I was at the church! Would you rather me be hanging out at a bar?" Civilly, he reminded me of the nights I had been gone the week before for church "stuff", and the week before that, and the week before that. I lashed out with everything I had, "How dare you say anything to me! I am doing the work of God!" This statement made him feel horrible, and I knew it. I had used it before. Because this wasn't the first time we had had this argument.

We had been married for 15 years, and for 15 years he had been competing with the church for my attention. Talk about me being out of balance. I was willing to sacrifice my family for the sake of God. Except it wasn't really God. There is a big difference between God and church. But I didn't know that. All the work I was doing for the church had very little to do with God. All the while, my family was suffering. I would go out and love on people who needed to experience God's love in a real and tangible way. Yet, my family was devoid of that love. Everything was out of whack and deep down inside I knew it.

Serving was fulfilling something else inside of me. Hear me when I say this: service work is good. But, we have to make sure it is coming from a place of overflow of the love we have first experienced from the Father. There is work that needs to be done, both inside and outside the church. But if that work cannot be done through a spirit of love, you don't need to be doing it. It is easy to recognize. **Ask yourself these three questions: Does it bring you joy? Does it bring others joy? Does it glorify God?** If you cannot answer a resounding, joyful "Yes" to all three questions, then it's time to re-examine why you are doing what you are doing. Let God lead you. God will make crystal clear what you should and should not be doing on His behalf if you are willing to listen.

I had lost all my joy. And not just in serving, in all areas of my life. When it no longer brings you joy, I can guarantee you it isn't bringing anyone else joy either. And if it isn't bringing you joy, and it isn't bringing others joy, it most definitely is not glorifying God!

I know all the concerns because I've been there. You are probably asking yourself, "Who else is going to do it if I don't?" This is the ego responding as if you are the only person on the face of the earth capable of doing whatever it is. If you are offended, then good, because that is a clear sign that it is time to pause. Trust me, God can handle it. Often, we think there is no one to do something because we've been doing it. But if you would step aside, you would be amazed at who steps up and how well they can do what you've been doing. Be careful here, because our ego steps in and wants to criticize, saying things like, "No one could ever do it as well as I did it." The ego has a way of twisting things around. Stepping aside should bring you joy, not jealousy. We don't want to let go of the work, the event, the fundraiser because it makes us feel important. We don't want someone to do it better because it might make us look bad. If these ideas bother you, it is time to re-examine why you are doing what you are doing. We are all working for the greater good. But because the ego is self-centered, the ego doesn't work for God; the ego works for itself.

I have always loved to serve. But the ego will make it all about me. "Look at me. Look at what I'm doing". This makes my ego feel pretty good. And then it becomes competition. "This is what I'm doing. What are you doing?" "You're doing that? Well, I'm doing this." I see it all the time. Not just in church, but everywhere. The fake self or ego is great about making you feel good about yourself. Often, the fake self will promote what you are doing, raising you up just a little higher than the other person. The fake self is sneaky. I've always been one to rush in and save the day. The ego loves to be the savior. If there is a problem, a situation, a crisis, I can rush in, fix the problem, and save the day. This is the savior mentality. It's the ego's worst work, disguised as its best. Dr. Wayne Dyer, in his movie *The Shift*,[27] talks a lot about the ego. He refers

---

[27] Dr. Wayne Dyer, The movie, "The Shift".

to it as "Edging God Out – E-G-O." That is exactly what the ego does. It makes it more about me and less about God. The self in me inflates, taking up more space, leaving very little room for God.

So, back to Travis and me. Because of our day-to-day challenges, I retreated to the church. It was a safer place for me. Service work became my escape. I could get lost in the work and hide out. Plus, I knew I was doing good work. It looked good, it felt good, and I felt good when I was doing it. Therefore, I could forget what was going on at home. Whether I could admit it or not, I knew that things were not quite right there. My work with the church helped me ignore my problems at home. Therefore, I just kept doing what I was doing, ignoring what was really going on.

I see this a lot today. We are so busy running here and there. If you have kids, that just adds an extra layer of busy. But here's what happens. We begin to hide in our busy. Our busy becomes our safe place. This is an illusion, though, and far from safe. It's a hideout and a way to ignore the issues at hand. You are moving at such a fast pace that you don't have to feel. You can just keep moving from one event to the next. And you can look good while doing it. No one is the wiser that your interior life and/or your home life is a wreck.

Maybe you are just numb. This is a dangerous place to be, the place where you feel nothing. When we begin to slow down, we begin to feel. When we begin to feel, we might feel like something is not right. If we feel like something is not right, then we might need to do something about it. Address the issue. Don't be afraid to slow down and feel your feelings. Our ego convinces us that everything is okay, that this is just life. You have to keep up. This is just the way it is. The ego convinces us that it is easier to ignore the problem. That it would be too hard to address it, too hard to try to fix it. Just keep moving, and you won't have to deal with it.

The issues that you are running from will not go away. Trust me, it is far better to just stop. Breathe. Look at the problem or the issue and see it for what it is. The ego keeps you in a place of fear as if to acknowledge the problem would kill you. This is a lie. The ego lies to us all the time. We are not meant to live this way, this busy, busy way of non-feeling. This is not living. We have forgotten who God created us to be. I was using the church and my busy-ness as a hideout. There was an emptiness inside of me, a hole in my soul. All the busy and the church stuff was not going to fill it. But I just kept trying. More church, more work, more service.

For you, it might not be busy-ness, and it might not be church. It might be a sadness that you know is there but are not sure why. Maybe you have everything you ever wanted in life, but you are sad. Maybe it is sadness of a lost dream or a life that didn't quite turn out the way you thought it would. You could be lonely but can't explain why because you have 998 Facebook friends. But you know enough to know that something is missing. That feeling is not going to go away on its own. God is waiting for you to come and uncover whatever it is. Don't be afraid of it. Uncover it and see it for what it is. Then you can be healed. Back then, I thought it was best to just ignore the problem and keep moving. I'm not going to lie to you; this did not work out well for me. Yet, the lowest time of my life became the best worst thing that could have ever happened to me, my marriage, and my family. It forced me to slow down. From there, God began to rebalance my life and my marriage and my family. I think God re-balanced my soul.

I want to ask you some hard questions:

1. **Why do you do what you do? Do you know? Can you guess?**

Jumpstart:

I would encourage you to do a free-flow writing exercise here, which means just start writing. Write out the question: Why do I do what I do, and just keep going. It could be a response to this chapter content and how it makes you feel. Or a reflection of your life. Don't spend too much time thinking about it. Just write. Let whatever comes out, come out. You can go back and reflect on it later. No one will read this but you. You can be as honest as you want to be. You can say all the rude and unfriendly things that you want to say. Just write it out.

Just the Facts:

- **James 1:26 NIV;** Those who consider themselves religious and yet do not keep a tight rein on their tongues deceive themselves, and their religion is worthless

- **Ephesians 4:25 NLT;** So stop telling lies. Let us tell our neighbors the truth, for we are all parts of the same body.

- **2 Timothy 2:15 ESV;** Do your best to present yourself to God as one approved, a worker who has no need to be ashamed, rightly handling the word of truth.

2. List all the things you do in a day.

Jumpstart:

Think about what you do in a day and, if you are ambitious, in a week, from the time you get up out of bed in the morning until you lay back down at night. Study this list. If you would like to, sort your list by HOME, WORK, SCHOOL, ATHLETICS, SPOUSE, FAMILY TIME,

CHURCH, ME, GOD, and MISCELLANEOUS. Tailor this list to best suit you. Start noticing your columns. Are they balanced? Please note, the ego would like you to believe that a full list is a good thing and to pat yourself on the back. Don't fall for it. Look for things like . . . I spend all my time at church, and no time for ME or for GOD, or no time at HOME. Being at church all the time is not the same as being with God. Just begin to notice.

Just the Facts:

- **Luke 10:38-42 NLT;** As Jesus and the disciples continued on their way to Jerusalem, they came to a certain village where a woman named Martha welcomed him into her home. Her sister, Mary, sat at the Lord's feet, listening to what he taught. But Martha was distracted by the big dinner she was preparing. She came to Jesus and said, "Lord, doesn't it seem unfair to you that my sister just sits here while I do all the work? Tell her to come and help me."

  But the Lord said to her, "My dear Martha, you are worried and upset over all these details! There is only one thing worth being concerned about. Mary has discovered it, and it will not be taken away from her.

- **Matthew 11-28-30 NIV;** "Come to me, all you who are weary and burdened, and I will give you rest. Take my yoke upon you, and learn from me, for I am gentle and humble in heart, and you will find rest for your souls. For my yoke is easy and my burden is light."

- **Matthew 6:33-34 The Message;** Steep your life in God-reality, God-initiative, God-provisions. Don't worry about missing out. You'll find all your everyday human concerns will be met. Give your entire attention to what God is doing right now and don't get worked up about what may or may not happen tomorrow. God will help you deal with whatever hard things come up when the time comes.

3. **Review, reflect, meditate on your list of activities. Which of these brings you joy? Which of these creates stress for you? Which do you have no feeling at all? Is there anything you could mark off your list? Is there anything you would like to take off your list but are afraid to? Look closely at those things.**

Jumpstart:

As you think about the activities of your day, ask yourself three questions: Does it bring me joy? Does it bring others joy? Does it glorify God? Be aware that the ego will want you to answer the questions in a positive way that will justify why you do what you do. Be as honest as you can with yourself. Does this really bring me joy? Just because you realize something no longer brings you joy, doesn't mean you have to do something about it. We are just at the beginning of noticing things. Through the Holy Spirit, God will show you what you are supposed to do and what you are not supposed to do.

Just the Facts:

- **Proverbs 10:28 ESV;** The hope of the righteous brings joy, but the expectation of the wicked will perish.

- **Romans 12:12 The Message;** Don't burn out; keep yourselves fueled and aflame. Be alert servants of the Master, cheerfully expectant.

- **Psalm 118:24 NIV;** This is the day the Lord has made, Let us rejoice and be glad in it.

Prayer: Dear Lord, show us why we do what we do. Help us to see our lives with truth. Show us if there is anything that we should no longer be doing. And reveal in us who you created us to be. Let your joy overflow into all parts of our lives and glorify YOU. In Jesus' name, Amen.

Chapter Five

The Shredding of Self

DURING MY BREAKDOWN, GOD BEGAN helping me shed parts of myself that served little to no value—created parts that I thought served a purpose. All they did was inflate my ego. As the ego grows, the God-self diminishes. It is still there, but the fake self is suffocating it, leaving no room for the God-created self which has always been there.

A few months prior to my medical crisis, while participating in Pete Scazzero's *Emotionally Healthy Spirituality* small group study,[28] I read a story about a fifteen-year-old kid who ran into a classmate at high school. The boy became aware of his own self-centered behavior, having little to no regard for the well-being of his classmate. The story resonated with me because I had done the same things. The story read,

> "I suddenly realized that for the entire ten-minute period from when I had first seen my acquaintance until that very moment, I had been totally self-preoccupied. For the two or three minutes before we met, all I was thinking about was the clever things I might say that would impress him. During our five minutes

---

[28] Pete Scazzero, Emotionally Healthy Spirituality, 77.

together, I was listening to what he had to say only so that I might turn it in to a clever rejoinder. I watched him only so that I might see what effect my remarks were having upon him. And for the two or three minutes after we separated, my sole thought content was those things I could have said that might have impressed him even more. I had not cared a whit for my classmate."[29]

In response to this commentary, Pete went on to say, "What is most startling in reading a detailed explanation of what goes on beneath the surface at the age of fifteen is that the same dynamics continue into the twenties, thirties, fifties, seventies, and nineties. We remain trapped in living a pretend life out of an unhealthy concern for what other people think."[30] For me, this was not only startling, as Pete put it, but disturbing. First, because I did this all the time in conversation, thinking of "clever" things I might say, boosting myself, my attributes, my business, and my service work. Second, I have always cared about what people think of me. This was a double whammy. "Once you see it, you can't un-see it." I observed the same behavior in myself.

I could recount multiple conversations where my husband and I were talking about our day, all the while thinking of the things that I was going to tell him. None of which had anything to do with what he was talking about. I wasn't listening to him. Once aware, I would have to consciously stop myself, and focus on what he was saying. I am a work in progress, still struggling with this today. But, with the help of God, "I am better than I was yesterday and not as good as I will be tomorrow.[31]" Praise the Lord.

---

[29] M.Scott Peck, A World Waiting to be Born, referenced in Emotionally Healthy Spirituality, 77–78.
[30] Pete Scazzero, Emotionally Healthy Spirituality, 78.
[31] Anonymous

Recognizing this same behavior in my prayer life, I had to modify that as well. I would rush in, list all my needs, and rush out, with no listening. I'm not sure where I learned that conversation with God or others was me doing all the talking. Neither of these are correct. The definition of communication is connection between people. Webster's definition is "a process by which information is exchanged between individuals."[32] I was more on the lines of delivering a soliloquy, the act of talking to oneself.[33]

Fortunately for me, I picked up some new tools during my breakdown. Meditation and contemplation have become my teachers. They not only kept me sane, but both help me quiet my inner world. They have taught me to be a better listener when speaking with others and with God. It helps me to hear. I realized that when talking to friends, family, and co-workers, my mind was always rushing around, grabbing stories that would flip the conversation back to me.

Today, being healthier, I still struggle with the ego but in a different way. People come to me for advice, and I can offer it to them. This feels good to me. I must be very careful because the ego is still at play. I ask myself, "Am I listening or am I making this about me, the ego boost"? Listen first, then hear. Really hear what the other person is saying. To check myself, I use this tool. I say, "I think what I hear you saying is . . ." and repeat what I believe I have heard them say. This helps me not only in listening but in hearing and understanding the other person. My husband and I practice this. I might say something one way, and he will hear it a different way. It astonishes me. And yet it happens often. We are different people having different experiences. We hear and process differently, and that is okay. It is important to understand this.

---

[32] Merriam-Webster's Collegiate Dictionary Eleventh Edition
[33] https://www.merriam-webster.com/dictionary/soliloquy

THE ME DISEASE

The converse is true. My husband might say one thing, and I will hear it in a way he did not intend. Without really hearing each other, this leads to many misunderstandings. Sometimes all I need is someone to listen, to hear me, and to understand me. Other times, I need advice. We can't assume the other parties know which one you need at any given time. My sister and I practice on each other. If I've just spilled my guts about an issue going on in my life, I might say, "What do you think?" I'm asking her for advice. I have just opened the door for her to respond with her own thoughts. To assume that she, or anyone else, should know if I need her to listen, or if I need her advice, is unhealthy and unrealistic. Do not assume that anyone knows what you need or what you are really asking for. Practice clearly asking for what you need. Be brave enough to ask for what you need. We must begin to model healthy behaviors for others.

I used to assume things all the time, assuming others knew what I needed, assuming how certain situations would play out, assuming responses to questions and assuming their reactions. For example, I would rationalize, "I'm not going to ask her to help with Vacation Bible School this year, because she's got a lot going on in her life right now." I would assume she would say no, therefore I wouldn't ask. She, then, would get her feelings hurt because I didn't ask her, inadvertently excluding her. I assumed she would say no, but I didn't give her the opportunity to respond for herself. Now, I'm dealing with her hurt feelings. Assuming creates unnecessary conflict. However, if I were to dig down on this behavior, the fake self would say, "I'm doing her a favor by not asking her because I know how busy she is." But, go a little deeper, and I would find fear of rejection. A "no" feels like rejection because I'm making it about me and therefore taking it personally. I am assuming her "no" has nothing to do with her and everything to do with me. How complicated is that? The ego/fake self would tell me that it is easier to assume the "no" than to deal with her own response. This is unhealthy behavior.

Maybe I assume that my husband knows that I had a terrible day. Or that I have a headache and he should leave me alone. However, he's been working all day. How would he know I don't feel well? Whether I realize it or not, I am assuming he should know. This is ridiculous. Think about it. How many times have I assumed my husband should know how I feel at any given moment? If he hurt my feelings, why would I assume he knows he hurt my feelings unless I tell him. Don Miguel Ruiz, in his book, *The Four Agreements,* says,

> "We have the tendency to make assumptions about everything. The problem with making assumptions is that we *believe* they are the truth. We could swear they are real. We make assumptions about what others are doing or thinking—we take it personally—then we blame them and react by sending emotional poison with our word. That is why whenever we make assumptions, we're asking for problems. We make an assumption, we misunderstand, we take it personally, and we end up creating a whole big drama for nothing."[34]

This leads us into my next issue: taking things personally. Just like I was assuming, I was also taking everything personally. These two behaviors go hand in hand. If someone could not meet me for lunch, I would take it personally, as if I had offended them. They were put out with me and therefore declined the lunch offer. If I asked you to help with a service project at church and you politely declined, I would take it personally as if it had something to do with me. Maybe you were upset with me and therefore didn't want to help. Because it is me. I would scour my brain in search of what I might have done to offend you. Unfortunately, I care what people think.

I kept uncovering layer upon layer of unhealthy behaviors. I wasted a lot of time and energy assuming things that were untrue, taking "no's"

---

[34] Don Miguel Ruiz, *The Four Agreements,* 63–64.

THE ME DISEASE

personally, and trying to figure out why someone responded the way they did. Ruiz says,

> "We think we are responsible for everything. Me, me, me, always me! Nothing other people do is because of you. It is because of themselves . . . When we take something personally, we make the assumption that they know what is in our world, and we try to impose our world on their world. Even when a situation seems so personal, even if others insult you directly, it has nothing to do with you. What they say, what they do, and the opinions they gave are according to the agreements they have in their own minds . . . Don't take anything personally because by taking things personally you set yourself up to suffer for nothing. When we really see other people as they are without taking it personally, we can never be hurt by what they say or do. Even if others lie to you, it is okay. They are lying to you because they are afraid. They are afraid you will discover that they are not perfect. It is painful to take that social mask off. When you make it a strong habit not to take anything personally, you avoid many upsets in your life. Your anger, jealousy and envy will disappear, and even your sadness will simply disappear if you don't take things personally. As you make a habit of not taking anything personally, you won't need to place your trust in what others do or say. You will only need to trust yourself to make responsible choices. You are never responsible for the actions of others; you are only responsible for you. When you truly understand this, and refuse to take things personally, you can hardly be hurt by the careless comments or actions of others".[35]

My unhealthy behaviors were leading me to the very place I found myself. However, God will always see you through whatever situation you are in, even if you put yourself there. God didn't make this happen to

---

[35] Don Miguel Ruiz, *The Four Agreements*, 47–58.

me. Regardless, God was with me then, and God is with me now. Rest assured, God is also with you and will see you through, too.

There are other times in our lives, though, where God allows something to happen. If we knew the mind of God, we would see that it was for our own good. But we don't know the mind of God. We cannot possibly understand what God is doing. There is one thing we can be certain of, God is always perfecting Christ in us, drawing us closer to the God-created self that we were meant to be.

I needed to go through this dark time to draw me closer to who God created me to be. God needed to rid something inside of me that had become toxic. During that painful time, God shed an exterior layer of myself. It was not a layer that God created, but one I created. A protective barrier, but my barrier had become thick and diseased. It was all about me. Even in my service to the Lord, it was still about me. For me to realize who God created me to be, that barrier had to come down.

Many of the great writers of our time and before our time, discuss this idea of ego, false self versus true self. Dr. Wayne Dyer speaks of acting out of the ego: "Ego is simply an idea of who you are that you carry around with you." He also says, "The problem is that we have allowed our egos, the part of us which believes that we are separate from God and separate from each other, to dominate our lives." Richard Rohr says,

> "Your 'false' self is how you define yourself outside of love, relationship, or divine union. After you have spent many years building this separate, egoic self, with all its labels and habits, you are very attached to it. And why wouldn't you be? It's all you know. To move beyond this privately concocted identity naturally feels like losing or dying. Perhaps you have noticed that master teachers like Jesus and the Buddha, all the "Teresas" (Avila, Lisieux, and Calcutta), and the mystical poets Hafiz, Kabir, and Rumi talk about dying much more than we are

comfortable with. They all know that if you do not learn the art of dying and letting go early, you will miss out on the peace, contentment, and liberation of life lived in your Larger and Lasting Identity, which most of us call God.

It was Thomas Merton, the Cistercian monk, who first suggested the use of the term *false self*. He did this to clarify for many Christians the meaning of Jesus' central and oft-repeated teaching that we must die to ourselves, or "lose ourselves to find ourselves" (Mark 8:35). Jesus' admonition has caused much havoc and pushback in Christian history because it sounds negative and ascetical. It was usually interpreted as an appeal to deny the body. But the full intent is personal liberation, not self-punishment. Centuries of Christians falsely assumed that if they could 'die' to their body, their spirit would for some reason miraculously arise. (Because of centuries of body rejection, and the lack of a positive body theology, the West is now trapped in substance addiction, obesity, anorexia, bulimia, and an obsession with appearance and body image.) . . . Merton rightly recognized that it was not the body that had to 'die' but the "false self" which is always an imposter posing for "me."[36]

Many years ago, I wrote a poem about this topic. Funny thing, I thought I had titled it "Shedding of Self" but I inadvertently called it "Shredding of Self." I've included it at the end of this chapter. The word "shredding" is more fitting though. Shredding makes me think of tearing. In fact, the definition of shred is "to tear or cut." I wrote this poem probably two years prior to my breakdown. I hadn't gone through the lowest point in my life yet. Now that I have, shredding is accurate. Pieces of myself were torn away, cut from me. I could not be who God created me to be

---

[36] Adapted from Richard Rohr, *True Self/False Self* (Franciscan media: 2003, 2013), disc 1 (CD); and *Immortal Diamond: The Search for Our True self* (Jossey-Bass: 2013), 36–39.

without getting rid of these diseased parts. Yet, I clung to them as if they were my very life.

This fake self made up of these diseased parts had become who I thought I was. And if I created them, what of God's were they covering up? There is only so much room in this skin of ours. Anything that we create for ourselves is covering over the God-created self. Thomas Merton says it like this, "I love to clothe this false self and I wind experiences around myself with pleasure and glory like bandages in order to make myself visible to myself and to the world, as if I were an invisible body that could only become visible when something visible covered its surface. But there is no substance under the things with which I am clothed. I am hollow . . . And when they are gone, there will be nothing left of me but my own nakedness and emptiness and hollowness.[37]"

Shredding of Self
By Melissa H. Thompson

I must decrease so that GOD can increase.
Over and over again – Daily.
I think I am. But I am not.
I am is I AM!
The only thing I am is SIN.
Thinking of 'I' is sin. I must shred this 'I'-dolatry, this worship of self.
There is more to me than self. If I am to be, the Spirit is what makes me anything.
That's the spirit that comes alive,
awakens to the God self in me, that has always been.
This God self/spirit guides and directs me.

---

[37] Thomas Merton, New Seeds of Contemplation, 35.

THE ME DISEASE

Leads me.
I can do all things through Christ Jesus living in me
But nothing without.

This brings me to tears as I shift my focus for a minute, to you. You, on the other side of these pages. As I write this today, I feel you. Your pain. Your struggle. You. Maybe it's because I feel me, and I know where I've been, my pain and my struggle. I reached a place in my life where God was saying, "That's got to go."

I feel like I need a disclaimer here because this is where things can become distorted. Please hear me. I know there are those of you who are suffering with medical conditions, either named or unnamed, that will not let up, that will not go away. It has you and has had you for a long time. That is not what I'm talking about here. I do not believe God causes cancer or other diseases. I do believe God can and will work through disease. I do not believe God causes addiction. I do believe that God can see you out of your addiction, through the help of people and programs like NA and AA.

This is my story, and it's a hindsight story. It's a whole lot easier telling a story backward, where you see things you couldn't see when you were in it. Don't misunderstand what I am saying here. Every one of us is right in the middle of our own story. And every story is different. What is not different is God. God is real, and God is with you. If you get nothing else from these words, get that. You are not alone even if you feel like you are alone. God is with you.

So let me ask you:

1. **Do you notice any behaviors in yourself that might be unhealthy? Do you assume things? Do you take things personally? Journal your thoughts here.**

Jumpstart:

Think about the last time you assumed anything. Do you remember the circumstances? Think about the other party involved. Journal your thoughts, including the outcome. Reflect on this and ask God to show you anything that you might be unaware of.

Just the Facts:

- **Proverbs 3:1-12, The Message;** Good friend, don't forget all I've taught you;
  take to heart my commands. They'll help you live a long, long time,
  a long life lived full and well. Don't lose your grip on Love and Loyalty.
  Tie them around your neck; carve their initials on your heart.
  Earn a reputation for living well in God's eyes and the eyes of the people.
  Trust God from the bottom of your heart;
  don't try to figure out everything on your own.
  Listen for God's voice in everything you do, everywhere you go;
  he's the one who will keep you on track.
  Don't assume that you know it all.
  Run to God! Run from evil!
  Your body will glow with health,

your very bones will vibrate with life!
Honor God with everything you own;
give him the first and the best.
Your barns will burst,
your wine vats will brim over.
But don't, dear friend, resent God's discipline;
don't sulk under his loving correction.
It's the child he loves that God corrects;
a father's delight is behind all this.

2. **When you have a conversation with others, are you listening, or are you forming your response? Be honest with yourself.**

Jumpstart:

Think about the last conversation you had. Who did most of the talking? What did you say? Do you remember? What did they say? How did the other person feel? If you do not remember, were you listening? Begin to be mindful of your conversations. Listen first and then hear. Use this tool, "I think what I hear you saying is . . ." Repeat what you think they said back to them.

Just the Facts:

- **James 1:19 ESV;** Know this, my beloved: let every person be quick to hear, slow to speak, slow to anger;

- **Proverbs 21-23 The Message;** Watch your words and hold your tongue; you'll save yourself a lot of grief.

- **Matthew 11:15 NIV;** Whoever has ears, let them hear.

3. How is your prayer life? Journal what your prayer life looks like. Be honest with yourself.

Jumpstart:

Think about the last time you prayed. Was it a conversation? Who did all the talking? Do you listen to how God might be responding to your requests? How long do you pause? Thirty seconds, three minutes, 30 minutes? When was the last time you heard God speak to your heart? What did God say?

Just the Facts:

- **Ephesians 1:18 NIV;** I pray that the eyes of your heart may be enlightened in order that you may know the hope to which he has called you, the riches of his glorious inheritance in his holy people.

- **Jeremiah 29:12-13 NIV;** Then you will call on me and come and pray to me, and I will listen to you. You will seek me and find me when you seek me with all your heart.

- **Matthew 6:7 The Message;** And when you come before God, don't turn that into a theatrical production either. All these people making a regular show out of their prayers, hoping for stardom! Do you think God sits in a box seat? "Here's what I want you to do: Find a quiet, secluded place so you won't be tempted to role-play before God. Just be there as simply and honestly as you can manage. The focus will shift from you to God, and you will begin to sense his grace. "The world is full of so-called prayer warriors who are prayer-ignorant. They're full

THE ME DISEASE

of formulas and programs and advice, peddling techniques for getting what you want from God. Don't fall for that nonsense. This is your Father you are dealing with, and he knows better than you what you need.

Prayer: Dear Lord, forgive me for not listening to You or others. Help me to be quick to hear and slow to speak. Teach me to hear with my heart so that I might understand YOU and others. (Pause here in silence and wait for God to respond; this could be 30 seconds, three minutes or more). In Jesus' name, Amen.

Chapter Six

Lessons Learned

I DIDN'T REALIZE IT AT the time, but all that working for the Lord was actually just me searching for something. I knew I was not who I was created to be. Interestingly enough, the very thing I was looking for was inside me and always had been. But it was hidden, like a precious gem that needed to be excavated. Richard Rohr calls it "the immortal diamond."[38] You might be looking for something as well. And just like me, the very thing that you search for is right inside of you. Tucked away. Hidden. Scripture tells us we are created in the image of God.[39] If I ever knew this, I must have forgotten.

Rohr expounds on this idea,

> "'Image' was defined as our objective DNA that marked us as creatures of God from the very beginning, before we could do anything right or anything wrong. The divine indwelling was a total gratuitous gift, standing presence, and guarantee; it is the Holy Spirit living within us, sometimes called "uncreated grace."

---

[38] Richard Rohr, Immortal Diamond

[39] Genesis 1:27 NIV; So God created mankind in his own image, in the image of God he created them; male and female he created them.

THE ME DISEASE

> We were the containers, "temples," or recipients of this gift. In a certain sense, it had nothing to do with us, and yet said everything about our core identity. It gave every human being an inherent dignity, which I am calling your True Self and your immortal diamond.[40]"

Just prior to the breakdown, I had been doing a lot of chasing after things in search of answers to questions I had never asked before. Questions about my faith, church, God, family, and myself. The more I knew, the more I wanted to know. I searched for knowledge and understanding in all areas of my life. Solomon writes,

> "I thought to myself,
> Look, I have grown and increased in wisdom more than anyone . . . before me;
> I have experienced much of wisdom and knowledge.
> Then I applied myself to the understanding of wisdom and also of madness and folly,
> but I learned that this, too, is a chasing after the wind.
> For with much wisdom comes much sorrow,
> the more knowledge, the more grief."[41]

After the breakdown, I found myself in a very vulnerable state. I had lost a part of myself—that fake part that needed to be cut away to reveal the True Self. But I didn't know it. I only knew something was different. I cannot say it felt good. It felt like I was walking around naked in front of everyone. Embarrassed, exposed, and vulnerable. That's how I would describe it. But isn't this how God made us? Why the embarrassment? He knows our nakedness and our vulnerability. This was new for me.

---

[40] Richard Rohr, *Immortal Diamond*, 121.
[41] Ecclesiastes 1:16–18.

With this newness came something else: anxiety and panic attacks. I had experienced anxiety for years; I just did not know what it was. All that assuming and worrying over what people thought of me caused me to be nervous and anxious most of the time. I had never experienced a panic attack until after my medical crisis.

I remember one of my very first outings. It was near the end of the six weeks of my medical crisis. I had not left the house except for doctor's appointments. My husband thought it would be good idea to venture out for some fresh air and change in scenery. We headed up to the local Japanese restaurant. As we drove toward our destination, I noticed the warm sun on my face, and I closed my eyes. We didn't talk much. Silence was my friend and Travis knew it. As we struggled to find a place to park, my heart began to beat a little faster. We pulled into a spot and headed for the door. My mind was fuzzy, and my eyes began to dart around the restaurant as we waited to be seated. The staff rushed from table to table as people talked and laughed and ate their food. As they seated us, I quickly retreated behind the large menu, trying to hide the anxiety that was building inside me. As the noise in the restaurant rose, so did my anxiety.

As our drinks arrived, my mind kept processing all the sights and sounds. My breathing became shorter and a little labored. Travis noticed. My heart was beginning to race. My eyes had already found the exit door in hopes that I could just run outside and escape. Travis sensed that I was about to jump up, and he lightly touched my hand and made me make eye contact with him. I felt my throat begin to constrict. He gently slid his cola over to me and encouraged me to take a sip. He calmly told me to focus on the straw in the drink and encouraged me to take another slow sip through that straw. When I did, he asked me to breathe slowly in through my nose and out through my mouth, still focusing on the straw. His encouragement to breathe led me out of that panic attack. I was able to stay and finish my meal. I can't say I enjoyed it though.

THE ME DISEASE

This was the first time my husband saved my life. It would not be the last. Being a fireman, he is trained for crisis situations. When most of us are freaking out, he is calm and steady. He gave me his gift that day. He gave me his sense of calm, and he became my safe place. I began to appreciate Travis for who he is. I had never allowed him to save or even comfort me before. My fake-self had convinced me I didn't need help with anything. I was much too strong for that. Travis becoming my safe place was a bonus. God was righting all the things that I had turned upside down: rebalancing me, my husband, and our marriage.

Shortly after this, I would return to work. Stress just came with my daily work. On this day, it was no different. As long as I had my business, I had stress and lots of it. Stress plays havoc on our bodies and our minds in ways I did not fully understand. Just coming back from my breakdown, I couldn't seem to manage the stress load as well. On this day, I remember being flushed with emotion. I had an irritable customer on the phone and an upset employee in my office. I had always been able to control my emotions. Not really control but hide them. Something had changed. I was upset and stressed out. And it appeared I had no place to hide them. My barrier was gone. I felt my breath start to quicken. My fight-or-flight reflexes kicked in, and I only had one choice. Leave. Being the owner, that's exactly what I did. I practically ran out of the office, muttering, "I've got to go," on the way out the door.

When I got in my car, the anxiety didn't stop. It was like a runaway train. My breathing became shallow. I felt like I had a baseball in my throat and bricks on my chest. I cranked the car, fastened my seat belt, and headed for home. The feelings got worse. I could not breathe or swallow. I thought I was going to die. I sent a text to Travis to see if he was at home. Praying he would be by the time I pulled in the driveway as I was having a full on panic attack. I was relieved to see his truck in the driveway. I hopped out of my car and found him standing at the door waiting for me, with his arms opened wide. I fell into his chest as he wrapped his big arms around me. My body heaved up and down as I struggled to breathe. He calmed me with his words, reassuring me that I would not die. He told me I might hyperventilate and pass out, but it would not kill me. We laughed just a little, then I cried. Things were strange for me in my newfound self.

A few days later, I had lunch with a friend I hadn't seen in months. She did not know all that I had been through. I began to tell her about "my medical crisis." As I told her my story, I realized I had always stood in my own strength. Before my breakdown, I thought I was strong, and I would have told you so. I was a mother, wife, business owner, church worker. I was doing it all, and I thought I was doing it well. I never understood that verse in Corinthians that talked about "when I am weak." In fact, I thought it read "When I am weak then *YOU* are strong." I knew I was not weak, therefore, I could not reconcile this verse in my mind. The verse actually reads, "When I am weak, then I am strong."[42] How can I be weak and strong at the same time?

You must back up to verse 9 to understand what God is saying here. "My grace is sufficient for you, for my power is made perfect in weakness. Therefore, I will boast all the more gladly about my weaknesses, so that Christ's power may rest on me. That is why, for Christ's sake, I delight in weaknesses, in insults, in hardships, in persecutions, in difficulties. For when I am weak, then I am strong[43]" Suddenly, with a wave of emotion, I understood. God's power is made perfect in my weakness. In these brand-new moments of my brand-new self, I find God perfecting Christ in me. God's grace is enough. For years, I had been standing in my own strength, standing in that fake-self. Now that old self had been torn away. I stand in Christ alone. I have nothing else to stand on. That

---

[42] 2 Corinthians 12:10 NIV
[43] 2 Corinthians 12:9–10 NIV

THE ME DISEASE

God-created self, the image of God I was created to be, that is the only strength I can stand in.

It was difficult getting used to my true self with no fake-self around. Sometimes, I felt like I was walking around in someone else's body. It was all so new and different. I used to be pretty social and could carry myself in a crowd with no problem. I enjoyed it. It always gave the ego a chance to flex its muscles. If you know me, you would probably describe me as an extrovert. I am not. This is one of the things I have learned about myself. I am an introvert. I draw my energy from being alone. Extroverts draw their energy from being with other people. I never knew this about myself. After my breakdown, being alone was my favorite thing to do. One, it was safe. Two, I was becoming who God created me to be.

A couple of weeks after I went back to work, we were invited to a party. This would be my first social gathering since the crisis. I quickly RSVP'd "YES" because that's what my old self would have done, not stopping to ask if I even wanted to go. I often did what others expected of me because I'm a people pleaser and care what others think of me. It never mattered what I wanted. I did what was expected of me.

As the day approached, I found myself filled with anxiety at the thought of attending. I did not even want to go. However, we said that we would, so we did. It was at this party that I realized one of the things I had lost was my external barrier. I think we all have this defense mechanism, like a protective shield that guards us. It helped me to maneuver in social settings without getting beat up by casual conversation. It also helped to redirect the conversation back to me.

This barrier was gone, somehow ripped away during my medical crisis. With no protective layer, I was vulnerable in a way I had never experienced. The attendees at this party knew I had been sick; they just didn't know what had actually happened. People would ask me how I was doing. The old self would have relished this opportunity, bringing me to the center of the conversation. But my new self was naked and exposed. There was no faking it. The old answer, "Oh, I'm good," would not suffice. The words—the lies, really—would not form on my lips. The questions forced me to respond with truth, explaining that I was sick for six weeks and in the bed for seven days straight. I made no bones about it. I had a really hard time. I didn't say it for sympathy or attention. I said it because it was the truth. I felt embarrassed by my honesty. I'm not sure why. Jack Canfield talks about truth-telling in his book, *The Success Principles* and says,

> "Most of us avoid telling the truth because it's uncomfortable. We're afraid of the consequences—making others feel uncomfortable, hurting their feelings, or risking their anger. And yet, when we don't tell the truth, and others don't tell us the truth, we can't deal with matters from a basis in reality.
>
> We've all heard the phrase "the truth will set you free." And it will. The truth allows us to be free to deal with the way things are, not the way we imagine them to be or hope them to be or might manipulate them to be with our lies."[44]

The old self would have told an imaginary story of what the last six weeks had been like for me. It would have been glamorized or downplayed, but it would not have been reality. To admit I had been sick, and that we couldn't really explain what had happened, would have been a sign of weakness. Never would I have admitted that I was weak. This new self was very uncomfortable. In these new social settings, I was learning who I really am. I am still learning today. Learning to communicate in a truthful and authentic way was hard for me. But it felt right and, in a weird kind of way, it felt freeing.

---

[44] Jack Canfield, *The Success Principles*, 401.

This was just the start of my new self. I had much to learn about who God created me to be. And, the closer I got to that God-created self, the closer I got to new emotions and new freedoms like peace, love, and joy. My journey was just beginning.

So, let me ask you:

1. **Have you ever felt naked, vulnerable, or exposed? Describe that time. Why do you think you felt so vulnerable? What could God be showing you about yourself in your nakedness?**

Jumpstart:

Some of the most vulnerable times in my life are in conversation with my friends. I find it is difficult to speak truth when it seems that truth is the only thing that should be spoken. Have you ever held back in conversation for fear of being uncomfortable? I wonder what would happen if you pushed through that discomfort and shared, in a loving way, what you were really feeling?

Just the Facts:

- **Genesis 2:25 NIV;** Adam and his wife were both naked, and they felt no shame.[45]

---

[45] Note that Adam and Eve felt no shame before God or each other before they ate of the tree. There was no physical, emotional or spiritual shame in their nakedness. Why are

- **Job 1:21 NLT;** "I came naked from my mother's womb, and I will be naked when I leave.
  The Lord gave me what I had,
  and the Lord has taken it away.
  Praise the name of the Lord!

- **Ephesians 4:15-16 The Message;** No prolonged infancies among us, please.

  We'll not tolerate babes in the woods, small children who are an easy mark for impostors. God wants us to grow up, to know the whole truth and tell it in love—like Christ in everything. We take our lead from Christ, who is the source of everything we do.

  He keeps us in step with each other.

  His very breath and blood flow through us, nourishing us so that we will grow up healthy in God, robust in love.

2. **Are there areas in your life that need to be re-balanced?**

Jumpstart:

Think about the areas in your life that might need to be re-balanced. List the first thing that pops in your head. Pray about this area and ask God to show you how it might be out of balance. Ask God to re-balance it for you. Journal your thoughts and be sure to date your entries so that you can come back later to reflect.

---

shame and nakedness now associated with each other? How would it be to live in a place of no shame?

Just the Facts:

- **John 8:31-32 NIV;** Jesus said, "If you hold to my teaching, you are really my disciples. Then you will know the truth, and the truth will set you free."

- **Matthew 6:33-34 ESV;** But seek first the kingdom of God and his righteousness, and all these things will be added to you. "Therefore do not be anxious about tomorrow, for tomorrow will be anxious for itself. Sufficient for the day is its own trouble.

- **2 Timothy 1:7 NLT;** For God has not given us a spirit of fear and timidity, but of power, love, and self-discipline.

- **Romans 12:2 ESV;** Do not be conformed to this world, but be transformed by the renewal of your mind, that by testing you may discern what is the will of God, what is good and acceptable and perfect.

3. **Would you consider yourself to be strong? Think about one of your weakest moments. Journal about it here.**

Jumpstart:

For me, it was difficult to understand the scripture, "When I am weak then I am strong." It wasn't until after my breakdown that I began to understand the meaning of this verse and how it is only God living in me that gives me any kind of strength at all. What does this verse mean to you?

Just the Facts:

- **2 Corinthians 12:9-10 NIV;** "My grace is sufficient for you, for my power is made perfect in weakness." Therefore I will boast all the more gladly about my weaknesses, so that Christ's power may rest on me. That is why, for Christ's sake, I delight in weaknesses, in insults, in hardships, in persecutions, in difficulties. For when I am weak, then I am strong.

- **2 Corinthians 12:9-10 Amplified Version;** "My grace is sufficient for you [My loving-kindness and My mercy are more than enough—always available—regardless of the situation]; for [My] power is being perfected [and is completed and shows itself most effectively] in [your] weakness." Therefore, I will all the more gladly boast in my weaknesses, so that the power of Christ [may completely enfold me and] may dwell in me. So I am well pleased with weaknesses, with insults, with distresses, with persecutions, and with difficulties, for the sake of Christ; for when I am weak [in human strength], then I am strong [truly able, truly powerful, truly drawing from God's strength].

- **2 Corinthians 12:9-10 The Message;** My grace is enough; it's all you need. My strength comes into its own in your weakness. Once I heard that, I was glad to let it happen. I quit focusing on the handicap and began appreciating the gift. It was a case of Christ's strength moving in on my weakness. Now I take limitations in stride, and with good cheer, these limitations that cut me down to size—abuse, accidents, opposition, bad breaks. I just let Christ take over! And so the weaker I get, the stronger I become.

THE ME DISEASE

Prayer: Dear Lord, thank you that your grace is enough. Thank you that you know us in our nakedness. Thank you that you did not give us a spirit of fear but of love and power and self-control. Re-balance the areas of our lives that need to be rebalanced. Help us to find freedom in truth and to always speak truth in love. Thank you that you are perfecting me in my weakness. In Jesus' Name, Amen.

Chapter Seven

The True Self Emerges

I WISH I COULD TELL you how I got a better, but I can't. One day, all those symptoms of dizziness, light and sound irritation, and vertigo just began to lift. And little by little, I came out of the darkest days of my life.

As my true self continued to emerge after the breakdown, I was amazed at the new feelings, emotions, and thoughts I was beginning to have. In learning who I really am, I realized I never had any empathy for other people. This seems odd to me, sad even, because I have been helping people for years. What I had for others was compassion and often sympathy, but not empathy. There is a big difference. I often listened with the intent of helping or fixing the other person.

The definition of compassion is "sympathetic consciousness of others' distress together with a desire to alleviate it." When I am sympathetic to another person's problem with the sole desire to fix it, there is a problem. And it is not the other person. This falls back into that "savior" mentality I spoke of earlier and has little to do with other people and lots to do with me. Just another attempt to boost the ego. Helping others makes my fake-self feel good and has little to do with the other person. However, after my breakdown, I had this new feeling emerging. Empathy. I was in such a raw state, that I could feel other people's feelings, not knowing that this is the definition of empathy.

The definition of empathy is:

> "the action of understanding, being aware of, being sensitive to, and vicariously experiencing the feelings, thoughts, and experience of another of either the past or present without having the feelings, thoughts, and experience fully communicated in an objectively explicit manner; also: the capacity for this."[46]

In other words, empathy is to feel what another person is feeling when you yourself have never experienced what they are going through. To feel their feelings.

I have a dear friend who has suffered with undiagnosed pain for years. I have always been compassionate toward her situation and even sympathetic. We have had long talks, discussing possible remedies, oils, soaks, vitamins, acupuncture, and yoga. We have brainstormed doctors' recommendations and prescriptions. I find myself wanting to help her, to fix her. I cannot fix her. Before my breakdown, I stood in my own strength. I viewed other people's problems as a sign of deficiency in their faith. I saw mental illness as weakness. I could not understand it or relate to it in any way. I believed pain without diagnosis was in the person's head.

Armed with my own experiences, I can now understand some of what my friend is going through. My symptoms manifested in a tangible way, in both my body and mind. It took me having that breakdown before I could empathize. I began to feel her feelings. I began to understand her on a deeper level. I could see myself in her. God was revealing in me my own weaknesses.

---

[46] https://www.merriam-webster.com/dictionary/empathy

For six weeks, I was in the bed, sick, and no one could tell us what was happening to me. I thought I might go crazy not knowing. My friend has been dealing with her own undiagnosed pain for years. Before, I could not relate to others who suffered with mental illness, depression, and chronic pain. Now, I can relate to those who suffer with mental illness, anxiety, depression, panic attacks, and undiagnosed pain. This is a gift God gave me.

I no longer want to fix my friend, I want to be with my friend. I want her to know that I am here for her. When she tells me about her day of pain and frustration with the doctors, I can say, "I understand," or "I am here for you." I can relate in a way I never could before. I don't have to offer solutions or advice. I have learned how to just be. This connects us on a deeper level. She doesn't have to pretend that everything is all right, and I don't have to pretend that I have all the answers. We can just be together. And together is a good place to be.

Brene' Brown describes empathy in a beautiful YouTube short. She says, "Empathy fuels connection. Sympathy drives disconnection. Empathy is this sacred space that says, 'Hey, I know what it's like down here, and you are not alone.' Empathy is a choice, and it's a vulnerable choice. Because, in order to connect with you, I have to connect with something in myself that knows that feeling. The truth is, rarely can a response make something better. What makes something better is connection."[47]

My compassion and compulsion to fix people was causing disconnection. All I ever longed for was a real connection with other people. Ironically, our behaviors often cause the opposite result of what we truly long for. It is important to be aware of our own behaviors. We must learn to become aware of what we say, how we respond, and our tone in the response.

---

[47] Dr. Brene' Brown's RSA Animated YouTube Short on Empathy; https://www.youtube.com/watch?v=1Evwgu369Jw.

THE ME DISEASE

I have another friend who I met a few years back. She has become the light of my life. When I first met her, I was in that fixing mode, and I thought I could help her. She suffers from noticeable fetal alcohol syndrome, with a cleft lip and shorter limbs. She has no family to speak of.

The first time I met her, she hopped out of her seat and hugged me as soon as we were introduced. She looked up at me, and, in mid-hug, asked if I would be her friend. Uncomfortable by her open affection, I didn't know how to respond. I didn't know her, and she was in my space. I wasn't sure what she expected of me if I were to be her friend. However, in my desperate need to fix people, I agreed that we could be friends. You would have thought I just gave her a gift. I wondered what I had gotten myself into. But, I knew I could offer her some kindness, and maybe buy her some groceries.

I had no idea that I needed her more than she needed me. She is quite capable of living, moving, and operating through this thing we call life. She didn't need me to fix her. She didn't need me for anything more than friendship. She exudes light, love, and a childlike faith that I had forgotten existed. She taught me that "friend" means talking about our day over hamburgers and fries. Friend means having a companion you can joke and laugh with. Friend means listening just to listen and hugging often. Friend means holding hands when you walk through the parking lot. Friend means love—that unconditional love that we hear about but never seem to find. Friend means calling just to say "Hey," and not needing a thing. Friend means browsing through TJ Maxx just to be together. Friend means going to pet the goats at the local strawberry farm and eating ice cream in the afternoon. Friend means being together just to be together. She gave me more than I could have ever expected. She taught me that God loves me, and God loves her because God is love. God is everything that love is and so much more. This is something I hadn't experienced before: Love for love's sake. With my new friend, I somehow found God.

Relationships and how we relate to each other are important. Pete Scazzero talks about our relationship with each other in his book, *Emotionally Healthy Spirituality*. He writes,

> "In 1923, the great Jewish theologian Martin Buber wrote a brilliant but difficult to read book, called *I and Thou*. Buber described the most healthy or mature relationship possible between two human beings as an 'I-Thou' relationship. In such a relationship, I recognize that I am made in the image of God and so is every other person on the face of the earth. This makes them a 'Thou' to me. Because of that reality, every person deserves respect—that is, I treat them with dignity and worth . . . True relationship, said Buber, can only exist between two people willing to connect across their differences. God fills that in-between space of an I-Thou relationship. God not only can be glimpsed in genuine dialogue but penetrates their in-between space."[48]

I somehow stumbled onto this truth with my new friend. I found God in her and recognized that she is made in the image of God, just like I am made in the image of God. When I am with her, that reflection of God in her is mirrored back to me, allowing me to see the image of God in myself. In this reality, we find true relationship. In this true relationship, I find God on a regular basis.

This idea of togetherness, oneness, is beginning to pop out at me. I am shifting from me to WE. It is a collective idea that we are one people—all of us. If one of us suffers, then we all suffer. These are not my thoughts. God is taking me to a new place. A place of oneness. A place

---

[48] Pete Scazzero, Emotionally Healthy Spirituality, 182–186.

THE ME DISEASE

of community. I remember something I scribbled on a post-it note sometime back: "Where is the suffering? Go there." I've kept that note for reasons I do not understand. But the answers are beginning to show themselves. I pray, "God, may we be the Church you have called us to be and may it begin with me."

So, I'll ask you;

1. **Do you listen with the sole purpose to fix or help the other person?**
   Think about the last time you offered someone advice. Back the story up, meaning, rewind the conversation back to the beginning. How could you have listened with a more empathic ear?

Jumpstart:

Often in conversation, I default to wanting to help or fix the other person in their current situation. I have to be mindful of myself. I have to be intentional on listening to hear instead of listening to fix. My husband reminds me that I still do this with him today. I am a work in progress. Journal about your last conversation and think about their situation and how you listened. Were you listening to fix or listening to hear and understand?

Just the Facts:

- **Proverbs 21:23 ESV;** Whoever keeps his mouth and his tongue keeps himself out of trouble.

- **Proverbs 17:27 Amplified;** He who has knowledge restrains and is careful with his words. And a man of understanding and wisdom has a cool spirit (self-control, an even temper).

- **Proverbs 2:2-5 The Message;** Good friend, take to heart what I'm telling you;
collect my counsels and guard them with your life.
Tune your ears to the world of Wisdom;
set your heart on a life of Understanding.
That's right—if you make Insight your priority,
and won't take no for an answer,
Searching for it like a prospector panning for gold,
like an adventurer on a treasure hunt,
Believe me, before you know it Fear-of-God will be yours;
you'll have come upon the Knowledge of God.

2. **Have you ever experienced empathy for another person? Journal that experience here.**

Jumpstart:

Think about a time that you experienced great emotion while a person/friend was telling a story. Maybe their story brought you to tears at hearing what they were currently going through. Maybe your rush of emotion surprised you. I remember being with some girlfriends one day, sitting around talking. One friend shared that she felt so alone most of the time. Her honesty and vulnerability brought me to tears. In that moment, I could feel her loneliness. I reached out and touched her hand as she continued to share. We experienced a connection on a deep, emotional level that day. Can you think of a similar situation that you experienced? Maybe your emotion surprised you. Do you think you were feeling their feelings? Begin to recognize empathy in yourself.

Just the Facts:

- **Ephesians 4:2 NIV;** Be completely humble and gentle; be patient, bearing with one another in love.

- **Romans 12:15-16 The Message;** Bless your enemies; no cursing under your breath. Laugh with your happy friends when they're happy; share tears when they're down. Get along with each other; don't be stuck-up. Make friends with nobodies; don't be the great somebody.

- **Galatians 5:14 ESV;** For the whole law is fulfilled in one word: "You shall love your neighbor as yourself."

3. Practice empathy with another person. This will be a tough one.

Jumpstart:

The next time you find yourself in a conversation with someone, detach from your mind and let your heart take over. Imagine how they must be feeling. Imagine being them. Can you feel what they are feeling? Can you picture yourself in their situation without trying to figure out what you could do differently? If this is too difficult, and it might be, remember the conversation and journal about it later. Practice in your journal feeling their feelings. Push yourself. Don't judge and, if you do, recognize the judgment, forgive yourself, and go on. Judgment instantly stops empathy. Be aware of that. This will be an exercise that you may have to come back to a few times, or many times. Keep going. Keep trying. This is hard stuff.

Just the Facts:

- **Philippians 2:2-4 The Message;** If you've gotten anything at all out of following Christ, if his love has made any difference in your life, if being in a community of the Spirit means anything to you, if you have a heart, if you care—then do me a favor: Agree with each other, love each other, be deep-spirited friends. Don't push your way to the front; don't sweet-talk your way to the top. Put yourself aside and help others get ahead. Don't be obsessed with getting your own advantage. Forget yourselves long enough to lend a helping hand.

- **1 Corinthians 12:25-26 ESV;** that there may be no division in the body, but that the members may have the same care for one another. If one member suffers, all suffer together; if one member is honored, all rejoice together.

- **John 11:35 Amplified;** Jesus wept.[49]

Prayer: Dear Lord, I confess that I have so much to learn about your love. Teach me to love like you love, to listen like you listen, and to respond like you respond. Help me to understand that it is not about me but about WE. That when one of us suffers, we all suffer. Continue to show me your ways and lead me on your everlasting path. In Jesus' Name, Amen.

---

[49] Why do you think Jesus wept? Read the passage and you decide.

Chapter Eight

Becoming the Disciple
The Shift from Me to WE

As I CONTINUED TO TRANSITION back into my life, I could feel something changing inside me, a shift toward a more authentic self. I was moving back toward who God had created me to be. I am a disciple, a learner, and a follower of Jesus Christ. That means I am the student and God/Jesus/Holy Spirit is my teacher. I am still learning. I have been a Christian as long as I can remember. Yet, I feel like I am just beginning to realize who God is and who God is in me.

As I look back over my life, I can see God's hand at work. God has been drawing me into HIM, and into myself all along. God created me and placed that God-image within me. Now, I am being drawn back to that image of God that is so beautifully hidden in the very place I forgot to look—inside me. I came from God, created by God, and, when God breathed his breath into me, that breath became image—the image of God living and breathing in me today. That same image/spirit/breath dwells inside each of us, created by the Creator. I am beginning to recognize it in me, and see it in others as well. We all came from God. From His very breath. All it takes is an acknowledgement of that God-image to wake it up. I am reminded of a song.

THE ME DISEASE

Awaken my soul, come awake
To hunger, to seek, to thirst
Awaken first love, come awake
And do as You did at first

Spirit of the Living God come fall afresh on me
Come wake me from my sleep
Blow through the caverns of my soul
Pour in me to overflow[50]

I wonder if I have been asleep all this time.

In Richard Rohr's book, Immortal Diamond, he points us to 1 Peter 1:3-4, stating,

> "By his divine power God has given us all the things we need for life and for true devotion that allow us to know God himself, who has called us by his own glory and goodness. In this gift God has given us a guarantee of something very great and wonderful. Through this gift you are sharers in the divine nature itself."[51]

Rohr goes on to say,

> "This objective union between humanity and God . . . changed people and offered them their deepest identity and form ("transformation"). We had thought our form was merely human, but Jesus came to tell us that our actual form is human-divine, just as he is."[52]

Because of this divine image living and breathing in me, I know that I am Spirit, just as God is Spirit. I am love just as God is love. This may be

---

[50] Songwriters: Jeremy Riddle; Fall Afresh lyrics © Music Services, Inc
[51] Richard Rohr, *Immortal Diamond*, 119.
[52] Richard Rohr, *Immortal Diamond*, 120.

my greatest lesson: to accept this great revelation that God Himself dwells inside of me. Through this indwelling, I am drawn back to my source. This source continues to reveal to me who God is in me. This indwelling is leading and teaching me daily.

Just like the spirit is teaching me, I have had other teachers, too. God has placed key individuals in my life to help me journey back to God. These people have acted as directional signs, pointing me back to God and the God-self within me. These mentors have taught me the disciplines of my faith—practices that were new to me, but now have become part of my everyday life. As I go, it is as if God hands me what I will need next. It might be prayer, lessons in the scriptures, listening, obedience, or fasting.

I have learned so many lessons. One sticks out to me: we need each other. As I learn these lessons, I begin to realize that the lessons I learned yesterday, I carry with me today. We should always be learning. In the learning, we will make mistakes. However, our mistakes become our greatest opportunities. These opportunities will show themselves in our lives until we actually learn the lesson. Once the lesson is learned, we take it with us, and move on to the next lesson. God, through life, is always teaching us. We get new opportunities every day to flex those spiritual muscles.

I thought God had abandoned me when I experienced my medical crisis. If I learned that lesson, that God will never leave nor forsake me, I can take that with me. Then, I will be met with a new opportunity where I can test that lesson and verify that I did, in fact, learn it. I will encounter a new time in my life where it would appear that God is absent. I can lean on the lessons I have learned and move on. So, even though I thought God had left me, I now realize that God will never leave nor forsake me. God is faithful, and God is good all the time. Even if it feels like God is not there, that is not truth. The reality is, God is always with me.

THE ME DISEASE

God is still drawing me, and I am still learning. The awesome part is that I can never get to the end of God. Maybe it is through my learning that God is drawing me. I do not know, but I keep going. There is an old Buddhist Proverb that says, "When the student is ready, the master appears." Every step I take on this journey of faith, God shows up through people to teach me a new and deeper truth. I have had Sunday school teachers, friends, family, and the unexpected stranger teach me new things about our Creator. Even authors I have never met, many of them scattered throughout this book, have been my teachers. Ultimately, they are all teaching the message of the Great Teacher, Jesus Himself. Jesus has given us everything we need to know about who God is and what a relationship with God looks like. Jesus modeled that relationship for us. The Father/Son, Teacher/Student, Creator/Created, Mentor/Mentee. It is all in scripture. What a gift! We just need to be willing to learn from our Savior and to emulate what he did.

Dallas Willard in his book, *The Spirit of the Disciplines,* gives us a good comparison about how we idolize athletes and want to be and act like them. But often, it is only the outward appearance that resembles the idol. We don't want to do the hard work that is necessary to be like that star athlete. He says,

> "Think of certain young people who idolize an outstanding baseball player. They want nothing so much as to pitch or run or hit as well as their idol. So what do they do? *When they are playing in a baseball game,* they all try to behave exactly as their favorite baseball star does. The star is well known for sliding head first into bases, so the teenagers do too. The star holds his bat above his head, so the teenagers do too. These young people try anything and everything their idol does, hoping to be like him—they buy the type shoes the star wears, the same glove he uses, the same bat.

Will they succeed in performing like the star, though? We all know the answer quite well. We know that they won't succeed if all they do is try to be like him in the game—no matter how gifted they may be in their own way. And we all understand why. The star performer himself didn't achieve his excellence by trying to behave in a certain way *only during the game.* Instead, he chose an overall life of preparation of mind and body—pouring all his energies into that total preparation, to provide a foundation in the body's automatic responses and strength for his conscious efforts during the game."

Willard goes on to say that what we do on a daily basis matters. We must forge those practices and develop the faith and the discipline that Christ had. He continues,

"Some of these daily habits may even seem silly to us, but the successful athlete knows that his disciplines must be undertaken and undertaken rightly . . . and what is true of specific activities is, of course, also true of life as a whole. As Plato long ago saw, there is an art of living, and the living is excellent only when the self is prepared in all the depths and dimensions of its being. This is not a truth to be set aside when we come to our relationship with God. We are saved by grace, of course, and by it alone, and not because we deserve it. This is the basis of God's acceptance of us. But grace does not mean that sufficient strength and insight will be automatically "infused" into our being in the moment of need. Abundant evidence for this claim is available precisely in the experience of any Christian. A baseball player who expects to excel in the game without adequate exercise of his body is no more ridiculous than the Christian who hopes to be able to act in the manner of Christ when put to the test without the appropriate exercise in godly living. As is obvious from the record of his own life, Jesus understood this fact well and lived accordingly."[53]

We must choose a life of preparation. We must practice what we preach. We must exercise our efforts to be Christ-like. These things won't come naturally for us. We move in the flesh, but we need to begin moving in the spirit. We need to learn to pause before we act, pause before we pray. We need to stop to listen to what God may be leading us to do. Stop and listen to what God may be speaking to our hearts. Once we hear God, then we must do what God asked us to do. These are the things Jesus did.

How can we act like Christ without the appropriate exercise in godly living? How can we respond to everyday events if we haven't first studied how Jesus responded to daily events in his own time? How would Jesus respond? What would Jesus do? Back in the early '90s, WWJD became all the rage. Many Christians sported the nylon bracelet as a reminder of how we as Christians should respond in situations. "What Would Jesus Do?" What would Jesus say? How would Jesus respond? Do you know? As Christians, we need to know. And we can find out. The scriptures are scattered with story after story of Jesus responding to life. Jesus, like us, is fully human and fully divine. He moved in his flesh just like we do. At every turn, though, he would pause to listen for his instruction from the Father. Once given, he responded with obedience. Everything he did was for the Father's glory, and he often told us so. We see this over and over in story after story: miracles, healings, deliverance, reconciliation, and restoration. Jesus is not just the way, the truth, and the life. Jesus showed us the way through living out his truth through his very life.

I believe we can live a life like Christ. God sent his son to be one of us, to be Emmanuel, God with us, and to show us the way we are to live.

---

[53] Dallas Willard, The Spirit of the Disciplines, 3–5.

Jesus showed us what a relationship with God the Father can and should look like. Jesus' relationship with the Father was real. We can have this same relationship with God. We then can begin experiencing the things of Christ and do the same things Christ did. This, in turn, shows the world who we are and who we are in Christ. This world needs us to be the Christ followers God created us to be. Jesus as our model is one of the greatest gifts God the Father gave us.

The gift of the scriptures is another great gift God gave us. The Word teaches us how to live like Christ and who God is. Of course, the scriptures won't read themselves. You can scatter Bibles all over your house, or carry a bible everywhere you go. But if you never read the words, you will never know all the riches of this great gift God gave us in *His Word*. The importance of reading the scriptures may never be realized unless you start doing it. Then you will understand what the scripture means when it says, "For the word of God is alive and active. Sharper than any double-edged sword, it penetrates even to dividing soul and spirit, joints and marrow; it judges the thoughts and attitudes of the heart."[54] It also says, "It is the same with my word. I send it out, and it always produces fruit. It will accomplish all I want it to, and it will prosper everywhere I send it."[55]

If you never read it, you will never know. Once you begin reading the Bible on a daily basis, God's Word will begin to manifest itself in your life. Then, you will see the importance of reading the Bible. When you encounter God, through His Word, you will be changed. Why do you think scripture says, "Remember your leaders, who spoke the word of God to you. Consider the outcome of their way of life and imitate their faith." It follows with, "Jesus Christ is the same yesterday and today and

---

[54] Hebrews 4:12 NIV
[55] Isaiah 55:11 NLT

THE ME DISEASE

forever."[56] This is God. God never changes. His compassion never fails. He is faithful and fulfills his promises. All that God has entrusted with the son, He has entrusted with us.

You may say God has gifted us with grace, and that grace came through his Son who died on the cross. And I would agree. But often I think we jump to the cross and forget all the life that Jesus lived before he died. It is in his living that we see His relationship with God. It is so important to look to Christ to show us the way. Jesus being fully human and fully divine is the most precious gift God gave. God not only gave that gift to His son, HE gave that gift to us, too.

The biggest gift that God has given us is the image of God that has been placed inside each one of us. Christ had that image and so do we. It is that God-self we have already talked about. The one I had but covered up with my own fake-self. That image is there and has always been there. However, often we walk around for years, maybe our entire lives, and never realize that image is right there inside of us. The image is a gift. The realization of that image is something entirely different. Rohr says, "'Likeness' was *our personal appropriation and gradual realization* of this utterly free gift of the image of God. We all have the objective same gift, but how we subjectively say yes to it is quite different. Seeing our daily unlikeness to God in ourselves and in others, the practical Western church could not go there. But it all depends on what you pay attention to. The contemplative dimension of the church allowed you to rest in this deeper truth, self, and Mystery."[57]

Rohr implies that we all have this "utterly free gift of the image of God . . . but how we say 'yes' to it is quite different." In fact, maybe it is a gradual realization of this image, an awakening of sorts. Maybe that is

---

[56] Hebrews 13:7–8 NIV
[57] Richard Rohr, *Immortal Diamond*, 122

what makes the realization of this image that much more radiant—that much more special. It is a glorious unfolding, like the slow bloom of a flower in the spring. The growth happens so naturally and slowly, almost unnoticed. Then one day, you look back and there it is, the budding rose, all wrapped up in new growth. Regardless, the mystery is in the acknowledgement of this image, which we all carry around with us. It is the yes to Jesus. It is the yes to God. God in me and God in you. We all have it. We just might not know it. Or maybe we haven't said yes to it yet.

After my breakdown, I felt as if I had discovered something. It took some time, this "gradual realization" that Rohr talks about. This slow growth of a flower about to bud. I was awakening to my emergent true self. First, I began to see the image of God within others. Then I realized that what I saw in others was a reflection of what was actually within myself. I have the image of God within me. Now, I was shifting toward the realization of "I am the image of God." What I saw and see in others is just a mirrored reflection of what is in me. Not even realizing it, I was saying "yes" to the image that had always been there. I was acknowledging the image of God. Then I began to see God, not only in me and others, but in everything. I no longer knew if I was the mirror or if they were the mirror. It didn't matter; everywhere I looked, I saw God. The more I looked, the more I saw. The more of God I saw, the more of God I wanted.

I began talking to teachers, colleagues, pastors, anyone who seemed to know anything about God. God was drawing me to a deeper place of understanding of who God is and who God is in me. Most often, they would point me back to the Bible. But not without sharing their own personal stories of their own personal relationship with God. Amazingly, each one was the same but different. Each one shed light on the God of the universe on a one-on-one personal level. God is personal. God is intimate. God is relational.

I began studying the scriptures on what a relationship with God might look like, and that's where I found Jesus. But not just Jesus telling me all the things I should or should not do. Not a list of dos and donts. I found Jesus in relationship; relationship with the Father, relationship with others, and even relationship with himself.

John 8 shows us some of Jesus's relationship with God the Father. It also reveals to us the Father/Son relationship and the Teacher/student relationship, with God being the teacher and Jesus being the student. Jesus says, ". . . I do nothing on my own but speak just what the Father has *taught* me. The one who sent me is with me: he has not left me alone *for I always do what pleases him*."[58] Jesus is the student. God is the teacher. God has taught Jesus, just as now Jesus is teaching me. Jesus says that he does nothing on his own but only speaks what he has learned. He only does what pleases God. But how can we be taught by God or Jesus? I think first we must learn to listen.

There is a passage in Luke where Jesus is visiting with Martha and Mary and others. He is not only visiting, he is teaching. From the Living Bible, Luke 10:38-42 reads,

> "As Jesus and the disciples continued on their way to Jerusalem, they came to a village where a woman named Martha welcomed them into her home. Her sister Mary sat on the floor, *listening* to Jesus as he talked.
>
> But Martha was the jittery type and was worrying over the big dinner she was preparing.
>
> She came to Jesus and said, "Sir, doesn't it seem unfair to you that my sister just sits here while I do all the work? Tell her to come and help me."

---

[58] John 8:28–29 NIV

> But the Lord said to her, "Martha, dear friend, you are so upset over all these details! There is really only one thing worth being concerned about. *Mary has discovered it*—and I won't take it away from her!"

As Jesus began to teach, Mary sat down at his feet. Being the place where the male students would sit, listen, and learn from their Teacher, this was a bold move on her part. This would have been offensive to the Teacher and the others only because of her gender. Women had their place, and it was not at the feet of the Master. They were to be tending to the house, the chores, and the meal, as Martha was doing. But here we find her at the feet of Jesus. I can see her, sitting cross-legged at his feet, eyes fixed on him, attentive to every word that came out of his mouth. Jesus doesn't discard her because she is a woman. He taught her just like he taught them all.

But Martha is so busy doing what women are supposed to do. With a house full of guests, including Jesus, who she already knew was indeed the Messiah, she had no time to sit. Having the Christ in her home was a big deal. Martha was irritated because she was doing all the work, and her sister was just sitting there. When she could not take it anymore, she pulls Jesus aside to make him aware of the situation. Gentle Jesus responds, with "Dear friend." I love this Living Bible translation. Jesus continues, "There is only one thing worth being concerned about and Mary has discovered it." Some translations say, "only one thing is necessary." Mary found it! To sit at the feet of Jesus, to listen, and to learn. That's it. Sit. Listen. Learn.

How many times have I been Martha? Busy doing the things that have to be done. It is not that I am doing unnecessary things. But Jesus puts it in perspective. Only one thing is necessary. All this busy-ness, all this doing, doing, doing is not necessary. There is only one thing to be concerned about, and Mary found it. My soul longs to be Mary as I thirst for Jesus and his teaching. Could it be that the God-image deep inside me is thirsting after not the reflection of God, but the real deal? My soul needs a replenishment from the original source. I yearn to sit and listen, soaking up the lessons that Jesus shares. Scripture says Mary "chose" to be there. I think Martha also chose to be where she was, yet she was resentful because of her choice. She was really longing for the same thing. Maybe all I need to do is choose to be at the feet of Jesus, listening and learning. To make Jesus and his teachings a priority in my life over all the other things that I think are necessary. To practice the way of Christ on a regular basis, giving up all other things for the one thing worth being concerned about.

As I continue to dig into Jesus' own relationship with God the Father through scripture, I see Jesus going away to pray in solitude. Mark 1:35, The Amplified, says, "Early in the morning, while it was still dark, Jesus got up, left [the house], and went out to a secluded place, and was praying there." Luke 5:16 of The Message says, "As often as possible Jesus withdrew to out-of-the-way places for prayer." Matthew 14:23 ESV says, "And after he had dismissed the crowds, he went up on the mountain by himself to pray."

His disciples who were journeying with him noticed Jesus slipping away. Sometimes he would tell them, "Stay here while I go ahead and pray." They wanted to do the things that Jesus did. They wanted to do them the way he did them, even when it came to prayer. Luke 11:1-13 showcases this very point. "One day Jesus was praying in a certain place. When he finished, one of his disciples said to him, "Lord, teach us to pray, just as John taught his disciples."[59] Each Master had a way of doing things. Attaching themselves to Jesus, his disciples wanted to do things the way He did them. His students were wanting Him to teach them, just as they knew John the Baptist's students were taught as well. But they didn't

---

[59] Luke 11:1 NIV

want to do it John's way, they wanted to do it Jesus' way. They saw that prayer was important to Jesus because He continually went away to do it. They saw Him living out his relationship with God. In this very passage, they are asking Jesus to teach them.

He said to them, "When you pray, say:

> *'Father,*
> *hallowed be your name,*
> *your kingdom come.*
>
> *Give us each day our daily bread.*
>
> *Forgive us our sins,*
> *for we also forgive everyone who sins against us.*
> *And lead us not into temptation.'"*[60]

We see Jesus sitting, listening, and learning from God. Mary, the disciple, is also sitting, listening and learning from Jesus. Then Jesus teaches his disciples to pray. They see Him praying on a regular basis. He models the importance of prayer in His life, showing His disciples that it should be that important in theirs. Fortunately for us, we have the scriptures to show us the way. Jesus is that way, and he lives it out in his real life. As the disciples learned, as Jesus learned, as Mary learned, so we too are to learn.

Prayer is a discipline. Studying the scriptures is a discipline. Sitting in silence before God is a discipline. These are all disciplines that we as Christians must practice. In these disciplines, we recognize the holiness of our God. I do not know if I heard this or thought this, but it occurred to me the other day that it is not the power of prayer but the power of

---

[60] Luke 11:2–4 NIV

THE ME DISEASE

God in the prayer. Don't get hung up on the prayer. Get caught up in God.

Listen. Learn. Pray. That's what Jesus shows us. Listen to God. Just listen. Learn from God, Jesus and others. Pray alone in a secluded place where you will repeat the listen-and-learn part.

These are the practices we must learn. These are the disciplines we must use daily if we are to be like Christ in our lives. We have to start doing the things Christ did. We cannot hope to be like Jesus; we need to practice being like Jesus. God is perfecting Christ in us through the image of God that has been placed inside us. That image that has been there all along.

---

1. Do you recognize the image of God in yourself?

Journal your thoughts on the image of God.

Jumpstart:

As you think about the image of God in yourself, think about the image of God in others. Can you see that God-image? Can you see God in other created things? I have a love of trees. The bigger the better. I think they are magnificent. I am drawn to the trees and have been since I was five years old. But I never really thought about trees before. Now, I appreciate their beauty and their majesty. As they sway, I envision them dancing and praising God. Journal your thoughts here.

Just the Facts:

- **Genesis 1:27 KJV;** God created man in His own image; in the image of God He created him; male and female He created them.

- **Psalm 8:3-8 NIV;** When I consider your heavens,
the work of your fingers,
the moon and the stars,
which you have set in place,
what is mankind that you are mindful of them,
human beings that you care for them?
You have made them a little lower than the angels
and crowned them with glory and honor.
You made them rulers over the works of your hands;
you put everything under their feet:
all flocks and herds,
and the animals of the wild,
the birds in the sky,
and the fish in the sea,
all that swim the paths of the seas.

- **Matthew 5:48 The Message;** In a word, what I'm saying is, Grow up. You're kingdom subjects. Now live like it. Live out your God-created identity. Live generously and graciously toward others, the way God lives toward you.

2. **As you think back over your life, can you see God at work trying to get your attention? Trying to wake you up? Write about a time when you know God was trying to get your attention.**

THE ME DISEASE

Jumpstart:

Think back when you know God was trying to get your attention even though you may not have been aware of it. How does it make you feel to know that God was with you? How does it make you feel to know that God has been drawing you into Him? When you think about others, how do you feel knowing that God is drawing them in, too?

Just the Facts:

- **Hebrews 10:22 NIV;** let us draw near to God with a sincere heart and with the full assurance that faith brings, having our hearts sprinkled to cleanse us from a guilty conscience and having our bodies washed with pure water.

- **Psalm 73:28 NIV;** But as for me, it is good to be near God. I have made the Sovereign Lord my refuge; I will tell of all your deeds.

- **Ephesians 5:8-10 ESV;** . . . you are light in the Lord. Walk as children of light (for the fruit of light is found in all that is good and right and true), and try to discern what is pleasing to the Lord.

3. **What are some practices that you can begin today in an effort to model your life like the life of Jesus?**

Jumpstart:

We see Jesus responding to situations all through the scriptures. Search the Bible and find key passages that speak to you in regard to how Jesus lived. Look up passages on "Jesus and prayer," "Jesus and loving others," "Jesus and the Word of God." Find out for yourself what scripture says about who Jesus is.

Just the Facts:

- **Luke 6:12 CEB;** Jesus went out to the mountain to pray, and he prayed to God all night long.

- **John 15:12 TLB;** I demand that you love each other as much as I love you.

- **John 1:14 The Amplified;** And the Word (Christ) became flesh, and lived among us; and we [actually] saw His glory, glory as belongs to the [One and] only begotten Son of the Father, [the Son who is truly unique, the only One of His kind, who is] full of grace and truth (absolutely free of deception).

- **Isaiah 30:21 NIV;** Whether you turn to the right or to the left, your ears will hear a voice behind you, saying, "This is the way; walk in it."

Prayer: Dear Heavenly Father, give us eyes to see the image of God you placed within us. Give us ears to hear the cries of our neighbors. And hearts that long to do your will in everything that we do. In Jesus' Name, Amen

Chapter Nine

Meeting Together
The "We" Emerges

THERE IS MUCH WE CAN learn from meeting together, especially one on one or in a small group setting. I am a big fan of solitude and silence, prayer, and meditation. I must be careful though, because while being alone to be close to God is powerful, being alone to get away from people is weak. It is not what we as Christians are called to do. Christ gave us the greatest command in loving others as our self. By design, it is not an easy task. But, if we are willing to learn from our Master, we will discover joy in our coming together.

Those hard lessons are the ones I remember the most, the ones involving other people. People can be difficult. I can be difficult. However, we need each other. We are better together and we are here to be Jesus' hands and feet, the true body of Christ. It is in our coming together that we discover our wholeness. The Passion Translation helps us understand it this way,

> "Just as the human body is one, though it has many parts that together form one body, so too is Christ. For by one Spirit we all were immersed and mingled into one single body. And no matter

our status—whether we are Jews or non-Jews, oppressed or free—we are all privileged to drink deeply of the same Holy Spirit.

In fact, the human body is not one single part but rather many parts mingled into one. So, if the foot were to say, "Since I'm not a hand, I'm not a part of the body," it's forgetting that it is still a vital part of the body. And if the ear were to say, "Since I'm not an eye, I'm not really a part of the body," it's forgetting that it is still an important part of the body.

Think of it this way. If the whole body were just an eyeball, how could it hear sounds? And if the whole body were just an ear, how could it smell different fragrances? But God has carefully designed each member and placed it in the body to function as he desires. A diversity is required, for if the body consisted of one single part, there wouldn't be a body at all! So now we see that there are many differing parts and functions but one body.

It would be wrong for the eye to say to the hand, "I don't need you," and equally wrong if the head said to the foot, "I don't need you." In fact, the weaker our parts, the more vital and essential they are. The body parts we think are less honorable we treat with greater respect. And the body parts that need to be covered in public we treat with propriety and clothe them. But some of our body parts don't require as much attention. Instead, God has mingled the body parts together, giving greater honor to the "lesser" members who lacked it. He has done this intentionally so that every member would look after the others with mutual concern, and so that there will be no division in the body. In that way, whatever happens to one member happens to all. If one suffers, everyone suffers. If one is honored, everyone rejoices.

You are the body of the Anointed One, and each of you is a unique and vital part of it."[61]

We are part of one body, making us one. Even though we collectively make up one body, that does not mean we are all the same. In fact, we are intentionally created different. No one person is any more or any less important than the other. There is a unified need for one another, recognizing if one of us were missing, the oneness would be incomplete.

Have you ever stubbed your little toe? It may seem insignificant, but if it were missing, your balance would be off. One day, I jumped out of my car at the mall with my flip-flops on, not paying attention to my surroundings. As I stepped around the concrete block where I parked, I snagged my little toe. Snagged is putting it lightly. It felt like I ripped it off. I was certain it was dangling by a small piece of skin. Surprisingly, when I inspected it, my toe was intact. However, my whole body ached in pain. I hobbled around for a week, pampering that little toe. Being so insignificant, I thought the rest of my body would not have been affected. Granted, we are talking about toes, and Paul is talking about the body of Christ. But the principle is the same.

We cannot overlook the impact we have on each other. I remember going to visit a friend at the time of his wife's death. Distraught with sadness, he sat with tears streaming down his face. I fought my own tears. His pain and emotions were so raw, it was not long before I was crying with him. When one of us is hurting, we all hurt. We want to help in some way, alleviating their pain by bearing their burden. By being there, we do just that. It is our gift. When we cannot do anything else, we can be there for one another. Do not discredit the power of your presence.

---

[61] 1 Corinthians 12:12–27 The Passion Translation

But what about the "least of these?"[62] Jesus himself gives us our instructions. We would be wise to listen to them. When one of us suffers, we all suffer. It doesn't really matter who it is. One cold, grey winter's day, after we finished preparing meals at the church that we would later hand out to the homeless community, I climbed into my car, noticing my breath as it hit the air. It was 28 degrees, and the weathermen were predicting snow. As I drove home, the stale sky softly released its first flakes. Gently, the snow continued to fall to the ground, clinging to the grass. A winter-white wonderland emerged before my eyes. Smiling, I slowly pulled up to the stop sign and took a deep breath. Snow always seemed to quiet my soul.

My joy of the new snow turned to tears, as my thoughts turned to Jacob, a homeless man I had met the week before while handing out lunches. His bed was under a bridge. I imagined what it would feel like to sleep, not only on concrete, but now in snow. I swallowed the lump in my throat as I pushed the thought back. Later that night, as I climbed into bed, my cozy comforter and fluffy pillow only served as reminders of what I have and what so many others do not.

If one of us suffers, we all suffer. No one person is either less or more important than anyone else. It works in reverse, too. If one of us rejoices, we all rejoice. Weddings and births seems to be the most joyous occasions. Weddings have a way of bringing out the best in us, uniting us in a collective celebration. As the two come together, so do we. We rejoice as the new couple rejoices. We smile as they smile, cry as they cry, and dance as they dance. We are created as one and are better together as God designed it.

We are here to model a relationship of love for one another just as Jesus modeled that love for us. This example reveals God to the world and

---

[62] Matthew 25:31–46 NIV

helps usher in the Kingdom of heaven on Earth. "Your kingdom come, your will be done, on Earth as it is in heaven."[63] It is just good to be together. When we intentionally come together for the sole reason to love and support one another, something mysterious happens.

Being United Methodist, I know a little about the founding father of our denomination, John Wesley. Wesley believed that we should meet on a regular basis. Meeting together was critical to our faith development and growth as a disciple. Wesley traveled around preaching the "good news" of Jesus Christ, forming societies, which are better known today as churches. From those churches, he encouraged class meetings. Today, we call those class meetings small groups. Wesley's classes would be no more than 12 participants. *Accountable Discipleship,* by Steven W. Manskar, gives us a glimpse into Wesley's method, stating, "The classes met weekly to pray, sing, and read the Bible together. Everyone was given the opportunity by the leader to tell how he or she had walked with Christ since the last meeting. The purpose of the class meeting was to 'watch over one another in love.'"[64] Today, we often experience this "watching over one another in love" through our small group sessions.

The purpose of the class meetings then, and the small groups now, is the same: accountability. Wesley believed students should come together and give an account of their daily walk with Christ. In this coming together, they would listen, ask questions, support, and help one another, as they were being formed as disciples of Jesus Christ. Accountability is critical to the development of the disciple,

"because disciples need the encouragement and support it affords. Giving an account of the week helps clarify the areas of strength and of weakness. The strengths can be affirmed and perhaps can provide

---

[63] Matthew 6:10

[64] Steven W. Manskar, Accountable Discipleship, Living in God's Household, 16–17.

inspiration to others in the group. The areas of weakness reveal places where prayer, support and encouragement may be given. They also indicate where growth is most likely to take place. In the process, each member is formed as a disciple of Jesus Christ. Accountability helps keep those willing to engage in it moving forward with Christ."[65]

This was Wesley's way—to strengthen and grow a disciple through meeting regularly, confessing struggles and praying for one another. There, within the Mystery of our Great God, through consistency and accountability, we, as Christ followers, find grace and reconciliation. Of course, being the Methodist that Wesley was, he had a method that he employed in every class meeting. Whether one-on-one or within the class meeting, participants would meet regularly and discuss their day, week, or time since they had been together last. They would share the areas of their life where they were struggling and ask a series of questions. If they were not inclined to share, the questions were designed to expose areas of weakness, encouraging conversation, which would lead to support. The only thing necessary to make this method effective was honest participation.

Once struggles were revealed, the group, committed to holding whatever took place in confidence, would encourage accountability to living a holy life in Christ. They would conclude the meeting in prayer and commit to pray for one another throughout the coming days. Wesley believed that meeting together encouraged spiritual growth in each other and would lead to the development of the Christ follower on a deeper level.

Think about yourself. How would you feel if you met with a group or one-on-one to honestly discuss issues you experience in your life? How would sharing your struggles help you? If you have ever been a part of a small group or had an accountability partner, you may have already

---

[65] Steven W. Manskar, Accountable Discipleship, Living in God's Household, 16–17.

experienced this. For me, the support given has been much needed and always resulted in growth.

However, there have been times when I participated, but not honestly. Not being willing to share is a hindrance to myself and my own personal growth development. Being aware of our own behaviors is crucial. Acting on that awareness and adjusting behaviors as needed is imperative. Small group meetings and accountability partners often supply that outside set of eyes to clearly see a situation for what it is.

Some of Wesley's questions include:

- "Am I consciously or unconsciously creating the impression that I am better than I am? In other words, am I a hypocrite?
- Am I honest in all my acts and words, or do I exaggerate?
- Do I confidentially pass onto another what was told me in confidence?
- Am I a slave to dress, friends, work, or habits?
- Am I self-conscious, self-pitying, or self-justifying?
- Did the Bible live in me today?
- Do I give it time to speak to me every day?
- Am I enjoying prayer?
- When did I last speak to someone about my faith?
- Do I pray about the money I spend?
- Do I get to bed on time and get up on time?
- Do I disobey God in anything?

- Do I grumble and complain constantly?
- Is Christ real to me?"[66]

The first time I was handed these questions in a small group of about four, I was startled. We were asked to skim over the list of questions and let the Holy Spirit speak to our hearts. Then, if anything jumped out at us, we could share our thoughts. As I read through the list, it felt like the Holy Spirit smacked me in the face. The first question I noticed was, "Am I consciously or unconsciously creating the impression that I am better than I am?" My throat began to tighten, as I swallowed hard and kept reading. Next, "Am I a slave to dress?" Uncomfortable, I felt my chest tighten. The Holy Spirit has a way of bringing up what needs to be dealt with. I have always made sure my clothes were in style, and my hair and makeup were applied properly. I dress to impress. If my hair looks good, I look good. I used to joke that you can always tell what kind of day I'm having by how my hair looks. A bad hair day was an indication of a bad day. As I continued to read through the list, aware of my discomfort, I became offended. Being pre-breakdown, my fake-self was running the show. It did not matter what my interior world looked like as long as my exterior world looked good. No one could see what was going on underneath, or so I thought. I could fake the rest. Aware that these two questions unnerved me, I believe my fake-self was showing its first signs of cracks in the surface.

If you are in a small group or mentor/mentee situation and you are discussing areas of improvement and you become uncomfortable or offended, pay attention. It is indeed a flag and most likely an area for reflection. Perturbed, I left that meeting with questions swirling in my head. Questions like "What's wrong with dressing nice?" "So what if I

---

[66] D. Michael Henderson, John Wesley's Class meetings: a Model for Making Disciples, 118–119.

like name brand clothing?" and "I can't help if people are uncomfortable because I look good. That's not my problem. It's theirs." These are all flags, especially the last one. Because not caring about other people's feelings is not right. It is the opposite of empathy and the opposite of what Christ calls us to do.

Jesus calls us to love one another. If something I am doing makes you feel less than you are, then someone needs to be checking themselves. That someone would be me. It also allows for an honest conversation. But, who is going to be the braver of the two; me or you? First off, I may not know my actions are making you uncomfortable. I have to be courageous enough to speak up. Second, you may not know why I have made you feel uncomfortable. Either way, if noticed, it is an opportunity to have a conversation.

Brene' Brown talks often about "leaning into the discomfort" in order to experience real relationship. She says,

"What our brain does not take into consideration is the need for discomfort and vulnerability in real relationship." You may want to sidestep the discomfort, but Brown says that doing the exact opposite, ". . . can revolutionize the way you live, the way you love, the way you lead, the way you parent . . . Take those conversations and lean into that discomfort and you will be amazed at what happens next."[67]

After that first small group meeting, all those questions and feelings needed time to simmer before my soul could be honest enough to

---

[67] https://www.huffingtonpost.com/entry/brene-brown-discomfort_us_56128675e4b0af3706e14cc1; Huffpost,
How Leaning Into Discomfort Can Revolutionize The Way You Live
"It's he or she who's willing to be the most uncomfortable can rise strong," says Brené Brown.
Lisa Capretto OWN

acknowledge that I dressed to not only make me feel good but also to elevate me over others. Oh, the ego is tricky, always trying to inflate. At the next week's meeting, I pushed past my discomfort and confessed my struggles with dressing to impress. I admitted I did so to elevate myself over them. Through this sharing, I realized I also struggle with my self-esteem. I was surprised by the compassion and grace I was given.

My honesty created an open atmosphere, disarming the invisible protective barrier around us all. As my defenses went down, so did those of others around me. We were then able to enter a welcoming space where authentic conversation and real relationship could happen. In our honesty, something mysterious happened. We found life, we found relationship, and we found each other. This allowed us to move forward in an authentic way, encouraging one another. All the while, God was perfecting Christ in us and through us. We were at the beginning of sanctification. Amazing things happen in "meeting together." I guess John Wesley knew what he was doing when he introduced those class meetings so very long ago.

---

1. **Have you ever suffered when someone else was suffering or rejoiced when others rejoiced. Journal those experiences here. Have you ever experienced emotion for "the least of these" that Jesus refers to in Matthew 6:10?**

Jumpstart:

Think about when you have suffered and/or rejoiced with others. Now think about suffering with those less fortunate than you. List the ways you could be there for someone that you may not associate with. How could you show Christ's love for someone you may not know?

Just the Facts:

- **Romans 12:15 ESV;** Rejoice with those who rejoice, weep with those who weep.

- **Ephesians 4:32 NIV;** Be kind and compassionate to one another, forgiving each other, just as in Christ God forgave you.

- **Matthew 25:34-40 The Message;** Then the King will say to those on his right, 'Enter, you who are blessed by my Father! Take what's coming to you in this kingdom. It's been ready for you since the world's foundation. And here's why:

  I was hungry and you fed me,
  I was thirsty and you gave me a drink,
  I was homeless and you gave me a room,
  I was shivering and you gave me clothes,
  I was sick and you stopped to visit,
  I was in prison and you came to me.'

  Then those 'sheep' are going to say, 'Master, what are you talking about? When did we ever see you hungry and feed you, thirsty and give you a drink? And when did we ever see you sick or in prison and come to you?' Then the King will say, 'I'm telling the solemn truth: Whenever you did one of these things to someone overlooked or ignored, that was me—you did it to me.'

- **James 5:13-16 The Passion;** Are there any believers in your fellowship suffering great hardship and distress? Encourage them to pray! Are there happy, cheerful ones among you?

Encourage them to sing out their praises! Are there any sick among you? Then ask the elders of the church to come and pray over the sick and anoint them with oil in the name of our Lord. And the prayer of faith will heal the sick and the Lord will raise them up, and if they have committed sins they will be forgiven.

Confess and acknowledge how you have offended one another and then pray for one another to be instantly healed, for tremendous power is released through the passionate, heartfelt prayer of a godly believer!

2. **As you read over Wesley's questions included in this chapter, are there ones that raise emotion or feelings in you? Pause and journal what you are feeling. List the benefits of meeting together.**

Jumpstart:

When I went back and reflected on the questions that disturbed me, I was unclear as to why these questions bothered me. I tried to dismiss my feelings, but the Holy Spirit was doing a work if I would allow it. Later in my prayer time, I asked the Holy Spirit to show me why these questions bothered me. It took a little time, but the Spirit revealed the issues. Go through the list of questions again. Slowly read them out loud. Pay attention to your feelings. Mark the ones that affect you even if you don't know why. Come back to those questions and pray over them. Let the Holy Spirit show you only what the Spirit can. Allow the Spirit to do the work necessary and open yourself up to it. Journal your thoughts before and after prayer. God will reveal to you any area that needs attention. These are growth opportunities.

Just the Facts:

- **Romans 8:26-27 The Amplified;** In the same way the Spirit [comes to us and] helps us in our weakness. We do not know what prayer to offer or how to offer it as we should, but the Spirit Himself [knows our need and at the right time] intercedes on our behalf with sighs and groanings too deep for words. And He who searches the hearts knows what the mind of the Spirit is, because the Spirit intercedes [before God] on behalf of God's people in accordance with God's will.

- **John 14:26 CEB;** The Companion, the Holy Spirit, whom the Father will send in my name, will teach you everything and will remind you of everything I told you.

- **Matthew 6:6-8 NIV;** But when you pray, go into your room, close the door and pray to your Father, who is unseen. Then your Father, who sees what is done in secret, will reward you. And when you pray, do not keep on babbling like pagans, for they think they will be heard because of their many words. Do not be like them, for your Father knows what you need before you ask him.

3. **Brainstorm a list of individuals you could meet with on a regular basis to discuss the questions listed in this chapter. Begin praying over this list of people.**

Jumpstart:

When looking for an accountability partner, you want someone who will speak truth into your life. That person needs to be honest and have integrity. This is not the person you go to make you feel good about yourself or who always tells you what you want to hear. This is the person who will hold you accountable to meeting and speak truth and love into your life. There's a link in the footnotes to help you discover your accountability partner and questions you may want to use when you meet.[68]

Just the Facts:

- **Ecclesiastes 4:9-10 NLT;** Two people are better off than one, for they can help each other succeed. If one person falls, the other can reach out and help. But someone who falls alone is in real trouble.

- **1 John 4:21 The Passion;** For He has given us this command: whoever loves God must also demonstrate love to others.

- **Galatians 6:1-2 NIV;** Brothers and sisters, if someone is caught in a sin, you who live by the Spirit should restore that person gently. But watch yourselves, or you also may be tempted. Carry each other's burdens, and in this way you will fulfill the law of Christ.

Prayer: Father God, forgive me for thinking of myself more than I think of others. Show me how to love like You. Teach me to suffer with those closest to me and those I do not know. Teach me what it means to be part of one body, the unified Body of Christ. In Jesus' Name, Amen.

---

[68] https://www.allaboutgod.com/christian-accountability-2.htm

Chapter Ten

Mentor/Mentee
Better Together
Me2We

AS I LOOK BACK OVER my life, I find myself in various mentor/mentee relationships. I realize now that God placed people in my path to guide me and help me grow. Even today, I still experience spiritual development as a disciple of Jesus Christ through meeting with others.

In the past, I have often been the mentee, a person who is "advised, trained, or counseled by a mentor.[69]" There is an old Buddhist Proverb that says, "When the student is ready the Master shows up." I realize now, even prior to my breakdown, I was ready to learn whether I knew it or not. However, my participation would be key to my learning. Winston Churchill said, "I am always ready to learn, but I do not always like being taught." Willingness to participate is a key factor in learning any lesson. My stubbornness has never served me well. Fortunately for me, I

---

[69] Merriam-Webster's Collegiate Dictionary; definition of mentee

was becoming aware of my behaviors, and that was a step in the right direction.

A mentor is an "experienced or trusted adviser."[70] Trust is key in any relationship. I am grateful God always positions me with mentors that have a deeper understanding of their own spirituality. Modeling their faith by how they live their lives helps propel me further in my discipleship. It amazes me the benefits I receive from meeting with friends and colleagues with the intention to grow in our faith.

I have never had to look far for a mentor. Many years ago, working in my insurance agency, a woman wandered in, exclaiming in a boisterous voice, "This is the day the LORD has made, let us rejoice and be glad in it!"[71] This being my mother's favorite verse, my ears perked up. As I peered up from my computer, I saw this woman with her arms lifted high in the air and a big smile on her face. I chuckled at her presence even though I did not have a clue who she was. The joy of the Lord was all over her and in an instant jumped onto me.

She proceeded to explain that the Lord had led her to me. She was certain I would be able to answer all her questions about her medical insurance. My office specialized in auto and home, not health insurance. However, my mama taught me to help others whenever I could, so I listened to her story. She was right about one thing—God did lead her to me, but it did not have a thing to do with insurance. Fifteen years later, Sue and I still laugh about the day she walked through my door.

We bonded instantly over our love for God and began meeting regularly with each other. I admired her enthusiasm and wanted everything she had. She was happy to share. She could quote scripture like no one I had

---

[70] Merriam-Webster's Collegiate Dictionary; definition of mentor
[71] Psalm 118:24 ESV

ever met before and prayed the most powerful Spirit-filled prayers. I was jealous of her boldness for God. I seemed to be learning just by being with her as she retold story after story of God working in her life. She taught me not to be afraid to ask God for anything and to be courageous enough to do whatever God asked of me. As our friendship grew over the years, she continued to teach me new lessons, like how to pray with expectation, the manifestation of spiritual gifts, and the power of the Holy Spirit.

One night, at the end of a women's meeting, circled up hand-in-hand in prayer, she prayed specifically for me. She asked God to put His Word not only in my heart but on my tongue. I hadn't asked for the prayer, but Sue and the Holy Spirit knew my desire. Boldly, she prayed with authority and thanked God in advance for already answering the prayer. Sure enough, scripture began to pour forth from my lips. Sue would float in and out of my life over the next 15 years, each time teaching me new lessons and giving me tools for my journey. I still joke about how she walked through my door that day and changed my life forever. Thanks be to God, I not only gained a mentor, but a friend as well.

Meeting together assists in the learning process and reveals God at work in other people's lives. Just like God is working in my life, God is working in yours, too. Through sharing of our personal experiences, I witness God at work in others. This is powerful. As I go along, the mentor/mentee lines become blurred, as the growth benefits are on all sides. It makes me think of the scripture, "iron sharpens iron."[72] Surprisingly, the entire verse actually reads, "As iron sharpens iron, so one person sharpens another." The New Living Translation says, "as a friend sharpens a friend." We need each other. Often we sharpen and strengthen one another just by being together.

---

[72] Proverbs 27:17 NIV

Just as small groups have their benefits, so do one-on-one accountability partners. These can be framed in the mentor/mentee role or just friends that meet on a regular basis to discuss and encourage growth in their own spirituality. Consistency, intentionality, and accountability are key. I would suggest finding a friend, small group, or mentor and begin meeting regularly. Track your thoughts, growth, ideas, and feelings. See where you are in 30 days. If it's beneficial to your own growth, keep going. Do not bail out at the first signs of discomfort. These are often indications you are on the right track. Growth is uncomfortable. Don't be afraid of it. Be consistent in your meeting. If you say you are going to be there at 8:00 am on Monday morning, be there and be on time. If the meeting is not important to you, it will not be important to the other person. Through consistency and timeliness, trust will begin to form. Trust will lead you to honest participation and that is where growth happens.

Looking back, I suppose my mom and dad were my first mentors. By their example, they have taught me how to care about neighbors and friends, what a godly marriage looks like, and how to grow old together. They also taught me to work hard, enjoy life, and what it means to be a family. They are still mentoring me today.

My dad has always been my hero. But my mama is my prayer warrior. She is still teaching me about the power of prayer and the Holy Spirit. Her life is a testimony of the life of Christ. As she rises early to be with God, she spends large chunks of time reading her Bible and praying. As I watch her pray over her sleeping grandchildren, she is modeling faith in action. By her example, she shows me that if I am scared, all I need to do is say, "Jesus, Jesus, Jesus," and mysteriously a wave of peace will descend upon me, and I can carry on. Whether she knew it or not, I have been watching. I am not that little girl who thinks she can control the wind or God anymore. Our kids are watching, absorbing everything we have to offer. As a parent, you are a mentor, whether you know it or not.

Later in life, I would take on my first mentor role with Whitney. Being 20 years younger than me, she asked if we could begin meeting on a regular basis to discuss life issues, scripture, and pray with one another. Quickly, I agreed. "When the student is ready, the Master shows up."[73] We were both eager. It was not long before the roles of mentor/mentee began to flip.

At the close of every session, I noticed my energy level had increased. As we discussed our struggles, she always turned to her Bible to see what the Word said. She encouraged me to search the scriptures for a deeper understanding. We would examine passages, looking at content, context and audience. We always ended our time together in prayer, agreeing on our next time and place.

I had much to learn from Whitney. Her eagerness to study the Word was contagious. She has a boldness to pray not just for others but with others. Her excitement for the work of God lit a fire inside of me that is still burning today. I was not the mentor. If you asked her, she would probably say the opposite. It does not matter, though, as long as you are both learning. "Iron sharpens iron, as a friend sharpens a friend."[74] We were living proof of this sharpening.

A common topic for us was how to speak truth in love to our friends and family. We searched the scriptures and brainstormed action steps. Ephesians 4:15 says, "by speaking the truth in love, we will grow to become in every respect the mature body of him who is the head, that is, Christ."[75] We applied this truth in our everyday lives by practicing real scenarios of what we would say and how we would say it. If I needed to have an honest conversation with someone, Whitney would hold me

---

[73] Buddhist Proverb
[74] Proverb 27:17 NLT
[75] Ephesians 4:15 NIV

accountable to it. When I would try to squirm out of it, she wouldn't let me, often praying for me to have the courage to have the conversation. She was strengthening me and building me up. We created action steps toward our goals, like memorizing scripture and sharing our personal story with others. We celebrated our successes no matter how small.

When we hold each other accountable in a loving Christ-like way, transformation is sure to follow. Accountability leads to action, even in our discomfort. Action leads to growth.

Accountability is necessary in any mentor/mentee relationship. Personally, I hate it. I do not want to be held accountable, and I do not want to hold someone else accountable. This is my own weakness, but it's important for me to realize. Accountability and consistency lead to growth and transformation. Find a mentor, someone who cares enough to hold you accountable for your actions and who can speak truth in love into your life.

Pastor Mary was another mentor I did not have to look for. Newly appointed as our pastor, she started teaching me the first day she arrived. She challenged me to "wait upon the Lord."[76] Waiting has always been difficult for me.

I was eager to attend The Walk to Emmaus.[77] But Pastor Mary encouraged me to wait on my husband. The spiritual retreat consisted of two weekends. The men go the first weekend and the women go the next. It is not mandatory husbands and wives go consecutive weekends, but Pastor Mary advised me to wait until he was ready to go. Irritated, I took her advice. I really did not believe he would ever agree to go, which made it harder to wait.

---

[76] Isaiah 40:31 KJV
[77] How to find a Walk to Emmaus community near you; http://emmaus.upperroom.org/finder/communities

Several folks from our church, including my parents, attended and came back with amazing stories of experiencing God's love. I was anxious, and Travis was slowing me down. But Pastor Mary continued to encourage me to wait. Issues you struggle with are often the very lesson you need to learn. She and I began praying together, listening for God's quiet voice to lead me. God showered me with His peace. Mysteriously, I became okay to wait for Travis. While I waited, I began listening to God. I learned that waiting is not passive. Waiting is active.

During that waiting, Pastor Mary and I began praying for Travis on a regular basis. We would pray scriptures out loud over one another. Travis and I began praying together as well. Three years later, he finally agreed to go. This was not me wearing him down. This was God at work in his life, changing his heart, changing his mind. I was unaware, but God was also changing me. Attending the retreat together gave us a spiritual experience that changed our lives forever. I am certain that if I had not waited on him, we would not be where we are today. Not to say we would not be in a good place, but I do think it would be a different place.

Pastor Mary taught me the importance of prayer. From that, I experienced the power of prayer firsthand when God changed Travis's heart and he agreed to go. I taught Pastor Mary something, too. I taught her that it is normal to hear from God. She used to joke that if you hear from God more than once in a year, you were doing pretty good. I was already hearing from God on a regular basis. I began sharing with her the things God would reveal to me.

When you hear from God, everything changes. Throughout our time together, I continued to share with Pastor Mary what I believed God was saying to me. Pastor Mary began hearing from God. Today, she is prophetic in nature, meaning she hears from God through prayer. She is a discerner. She can meet with someone, recognize their gifts and know what should be prayed. Together, we were able to share in each other's gifts, learn from one another, and grow into the people God is calling us to be.

Then there is my most unusual teacher, my husband. The funny thing is I was always trying to teach him something. I thought I knew more than he did about God, prayer, and the Bible, and that it was my job to teach him. Strangely enough, I was the one always learning something. Travis taught me how to love when you don't even like the person. He taught me how to listen, not to respond, but to hear and understand. He taught me how to set aside my stubbornness and to do it a new way, or see it a different way. He taught me to not be afraid to stand up for myself and others.

Being a firefighter, he taught me respect and the chain of command. The most important thing he taught me is how to love someone, and how to make someone feel love. Watching him, I realized that just as I was growing, so was he. One of the greatest gifts that came out of my breakdown was Travis becoming the spiritual leader of our household. He is, in fact, the prayer warrior for our family today. Who would have ever thought? But, that is what God does. God changes us, making us into the people we were created to be.

Now, we work as a team. If we do not see a situation the same way, it does not mean it is wrong. We can view any issue together, with both sets of eyes, allowing us to see the whole picture. We are better together. No longer do we fight against each other. Now, we fight for each other. We pray together. And when not together, we know we are still praying for one another. If I feel weak, he is there to help me. If he is having a bad day, I can encourage him. God amazes me in the power of us.

To grow as disciples of Jesus Christ, we need to meet, pray for one another, and discuss the scriptures together on a regular basis. Hebrews 10:24-25 ESV says, "Let us consider how to stir up one another to love and good works, not neglecting to meet together, as is the habit of some, but encouraging one another."[78] When we meet together, confessing our struggles to one another, we are fulfilling the scriptures. In this, we develop relationships, friendships, and community. It also gives us the opportunity to practice our faith—what we believe and why we believe it. In the sharing of our experiences, we see God at work in our lives and others'. When we enter into relationships with one another, we move outside ourselves and into community. When we move into community with one another, we meet God. This is the "Me2We."[79]

---

1. **As you look back, can you see teachers/mentors who helped you in the formation of your spiritual faith? Think about the lessons they taught you. Consider writing them a thank you note to let them know what they did for you, or how they encouraged you on your spiritual journey.**

Jumpstart:

If you are having trouble spotting your mentors along the way, use this exercise. Draw a line, and a dot at the beginning of the line marking your birth. Note the year. Move along the line, placing dots when you first began recognizing God at work in your life. Think about significant people in your life at that time. Place a dot where you began having a relationship with God. Think about the people in between those dots and what practices you were developing, i.e., prayer, scripture reading,

---

[78] Hebrews 10:24–25 ESV
[79] 'Me2We, logo created by Julie Wooten.

devotions, serving. Place the next dot as a representation of your next stop. You could have countless dots occur as growth moments in your life. Who do you see in between those dots? Who could you begin meeting with that would assist in your spiritual growth from dot to dot? Mark other key individuals as you go. Dot your next spiritual growth movement. Do this until you reach today. Project to your next dot and where you would like to be. See my line below.

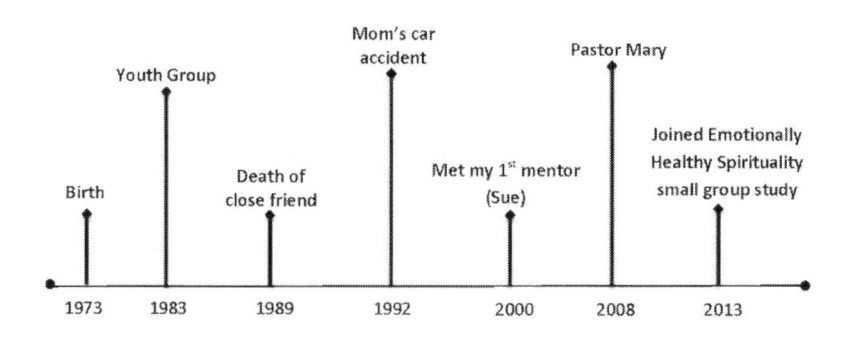

Timeline:
- 1973: Birth
- 1983: Youth Group
- 1989: Death of close friend
- 1992: Mom's car accident
- 2000: Met my 1st mentor (Sue)
- 2008: Pastor Mary
- 2013: Joined Emotionally Healthy Spirituality small group study

Just the Facts:

- **Proverbs 27:17 TLB;** As iron sharpens iron, so a friend sharpens a friend.

- **Psalm 32:8 NIV;** I will instruct you and teach you in the way you should go;

    I will counsel you with my loving eye on you.

- **1 Thessalonians 5:11 CEB;** So, continue encouraging each other and building each other up, just like you are doing already.

2. **How would you benefit from meeting with an accountability partner on a regular basis? What struggles are you currently**

facing? How might it be helpful to discuss this with another person? Make a list of potential friends, co-workers, and coaches you could begin meeting with. Pray over the list and choose one person. Reach out to begin meeting on a regular basis. What are things you could do to get the most out of this 'meeting together'?

Jumpstart:

When I joined my first small group, I was amazed at how little I knew, even though I thought I knew a lot. One of the areas I wanted to grow in was my knowledge of scripture. I could quote some verses, but I wanted to know author, audience, context, and address. This became a spiritual goal of mine. As I met with my accountability partner, we began to pray into this goal. This was an area that could only be fulfilled through personal study. Later, I found myself in a small group Bible study that specializes in studying the scriptures.

Just the Facts:

- **Matthew 18:20 AMP;** For where two or three are gathered in My name [meeting together as My followers], I am there among them.

- **Hebrews 10:25, CEB;** Don't stop meeting together with other believers, which some people have gotten into the habit of doing. Instead, encourage each other, especially as you see the day drawing near.

3. Think about how you might feel if you met with a group or one-on-one to honestly discuss issues in your life that you are

struggling with. If you have participated in something like this before, was it effective in helping you grow? If so, how? If not, why? What were things that you learned that surprised you? Were you honest in the group? If you were to do this again, what would you do differently to make your experience more beneficial? List specific areas you would like to grow in. What are some action steps you could take today to move toward that goal?

Jumpstart:

Find a friend or small group and begin meeting weekly to discuss your spiritual discipleship. At the end of each meeting, journal your thoughts and feelings about your time together. List your struggles, their struggles, and any prayer requests. Commit to meeting regularly, sharing honestly, holding each other accountable, and praying for each other. Do this for six weeks and evaluate where you think you are. Did you experience growth in your relationship with God? Commit to doing this for six more weeks. It doesn't have to be with the same person each time. (Use John Wesley's questions[80] as your springboard for conversation.)

Just the Facts:

- **Philippians 4:9 AMP;** The things which you have learned and received and heard and seen in me, practice these things [in daily life], and the God [who is the source] of peace and well-being will be with you.

---

[80] Reference Chapter 9, Meeting Together.

- **Deuteronomy 31:12-13 CEB;** Gather everyone—men, women, children, and the immigrants who live in your cities—in order that they hear it, learn it, and revere the Lord your God, carefully doing all the words of this Instruction, and so that their children, who don't yet know the Instruction, may hear it and learn to revere the Lord your God for as long as you live . . .

Prayer: Dear Lord, thank you for the gift of each other. Help us to see the importance of meeting together. Thank you that you tell us when two or more are gathered together in your name, you are there with us. Continue to bring people in our paths to help us grow into the disciples you created us to be. In Jesus' Name, Amen.

Chapter Eleven

Sanctification
Holiness
Perfecting Christ in Us

AS I JOURNEY THROUGH THE words, pages, and chapters of this book, I am amazed at all that God is still teaching me. These new truths have led me here to this place. I often feel like God is writing the book. As I finish one chapter, the next one is waiting for me. God continues to reveal His insights to me. The first is this: God is drawing me and has always been drawing me into Him. The second is just as powerful: God is sanctifying me. I thought I needed to do all the work, the discipleship, the service, even my own sanctification, as if it were dependent upon my own efforts. But it is not. The only thing I need to do is trust God and choose to participate in His work.

These truths are crucial to my discovery of God in me. I cannot discredit the work God is doing often in spite of myself. But as hard as I try, I cannot do the kind of work necessary. It is an inside job. This is God's work. Praise the LORD; it is not dependent upon me. God is and has always been working in and through me. He will continue until we reach that glorious day of perfection, all together in one accord.

THE ME DISEASE

As these two truths emerge, I am aware that there is no end to God, there is no end to this process. I am comforted in this truth. I hope you are as well. Because just like God is drawing me, God is drawing you, too.

The second revelation is almost too big for my temporal mind. As God continues the work of sanctification, I cannot fathom what God is doing in me and in creation. One thing I know for sure, every time I encounter God, I am changed. Every time! One of my favorite verses in Isaiah 40:28 reads, "Do you not know? Have you not heard? The Lord is the everlasting God, the Creator of the ends of the earth, He will not grow tired or weary and his understanding no one can fathom." We cannot fathom what God is doing or understand His work. Yet, I continue to try.

Even in writing, I didn't quite know where this book would end. I knew, through my medical crisis, I had a story to share of how God began rebalancing my life, including my marriage and my relationship with God. But somehow, in the retelling of the story, I discovered new depths of God. God is perfecting Christ in me. God keeps unfolding the chapters, just like God is unfolding my life. And God led me here to this place of sanctification.

When I choose to follow, God will lead me to new places, show me new things, and reveal my true self in the process. I am right where God wants me to be. Realizing this brings me so much joy. As I write, God allows me to glimpse the future, small slivers of time. I feel like I am back on that trail, asking my guide, "Where are we going?" and "How long until we get there?" God knows our earthly minds would be overwhelmed if He showed it all to us. God just wants me to trust Him.

These small acts of obedience lead us to our destination. Now that I am here, it makes perfect sense. My understanding of sanctification never lined up with God's truth. Some of what I knew was accurate, but there was one piece that was way off. Sanctification is holiness, perfecting Christ in me.

When I choose to trust God, God is perfecting Christ in me. It is in the participation that I find sacredness. If there is any holiness to be found in me, it is by God and God alone. In fact, the God-image dwelling in me is what makes me holy. God is holy, therefore I am holy. There is nothing to do. The work is done. I only need to accept this truth.

I thought my sanctification came through my act of serving. When I look back at my relationship with the church, any acts were done merely to support my ego. Serving as an act of sanctification is not God's way. Not that works are bad. Service should be an overflow of God's love within me. Working outside of that love, like working out of the fake self, has nothing to do with God and misses the mark every time.

As we begin to recognize Christ in us and others, we understand we are Christ. In 1 John 4:17, The Common English Bible says, "This is how love has been perfected in us, so that we can have confidence on the Judgment Day, because we are exactly the same as God is in this world." Awareness of Christ in us awakens that image. Christ begins to breathe, grow, and mature inside of us. At that acknowledgement, we birth Christ or Christ births us, the real us.

I always thought I had some control in this process, that my level of commitment as a disciple aided my efforts. But they were my efforts and apart from God I can do nothing. The only control we have is whether we choose to participate or not. When we say "yes" to that participation, we say "yes" to Christ in us. In that moment, we join all of creation in glorifying our Great Creator. "Holy, holy, holy is the Lord Almighty; the whole earth is full of his glory."[81] What joy we bring the Creator when we stand in the awareness of who we are created to be.

---

[81] Isaiah 6:3 NIV

THE ME DISEASE

A few years after my breakdown, I attended a spiritual retreat in the mountains of Western North Carolina. While I was there, God began doing work in me. While clinging to some fear, I proceeded to the prayer room at the close of the first message. Greeted by an adorable couple of 53 years, I confessed my fears to them. Hand in hand, we named the fear and prayed for God to remove it. After anointing my head with oil, they prayed a blessing over me and my life. It was short and simple. As I walked out the door, I felt lighter, knowing I was leaving the fear behind. Removing the fear cleared the way for me to receive everything God had for me that weekend.

The next morning, I sat silently in a prayer service surrounded by at least 50 others. As we prayed, God came and met with me. I saw God placing his massive hand on my forehead. He said, "Do not be afraid. Walk in the power of the Holy Spirit." It felt as if I was stepping into a sleeve of supernatural goodness. I pulled it up, like nylon stockings, from the tips of my toes all the way to the top of my head. Fully encased by the power of the Holy Spirit, I felt humbled and strong all at the same time. I hope I never forget the sacredness of that moment. Dazed and a little tingly, I left there uncertain of my experience.

Later that day, as I sat in a worship session with well over 500 people, God asked me to pray for the woman's knee sitting next to me. I looked down and, sure enough, there was a fresh scar on the woman's knee. Uncomfortable, I began pleading with God about why I should not pray with this woman. Gently, God said, "We can move as fast or as slow as you want to." It was not a rebuke, just a soothing statement. Comforted, it reminded me that we get to choose to participate in the perfecting of Christ in our lives. Even still, God is doing the work. God is drawing us in. God does not push or force Himself upon us. God is patient, kind, gentle, and slow-moving most of the time. As slow as God is, it seems HE is always waiting for me to catch up. As the service ended, I left the lady sitting there, annoyed at myself for not having the courage to do what God asked me to do.

The next day, I entered the packed auditorium for the final service. I scanned the aisles for an empty seat and quickly plopped down in the only one I could find. As I settled in, I glanced to my right and was surprised to find that same woman sitting beside me. God is so funny. Humbly, I explained to her what had happened the day before. I asked if I could pray for her knee. She graciously agreed. Before I could begin, her daughter piped up and said, "I think this is more about God doing a work in you than it is about this knee." Silently, I agreed, knowing she was right.

After the prayer, the woman disclosed that she had a mass in her upper left side. She explained while I prayed, the mass began to twitch and continued to twitch the entire time. The daughter, turning toward me, told of her mother's scheduled doctor's appointment later in the week concerning the rock-hard mass. Excited, the mom exclaimed, "Well it isn't hard anymore." She proceeded to pull her daughter's fingers to the spot in question. Sure enough, the mass had softened. I don't really know what to make of all this, other than God allowed me to participate in something miraculous, something I refused to take part in the day before. God let me catch up, and I am so grateful He did. That experience changed me. When you participate in the awesomeness of our God, there is only one response. Praise!

Merton talks about when we choose to participate, we discover God and, thus, discover ourselves.

> "Our discovery of God is, in a way, God's discovery of us . . .
>
> In order to know and love God as He is, we must have God dwelling in us in a new way . . .

> God bridges the infinite distances between Himself and the spirits created to love Him, by supernatural missions of His own life. The Father, dwelling in the depths of all things and in my own depths, communicates to me His Word and His Spirit. Receiving them I am drawn into His own life and know God in His own Love, being one with Him in His own Son.
>
> My discovery of my identity begins and is perfected in these missions, because it is in them that God Himself, bearing in Himself the secret of who I am, begins to live in me not only as my Creator but as my other and true self."[82]

By participating, we find sanctification, which unlocks the door to who we are. As God reveals Himself to us, we long to know God more. When I choose not to participate, God is still working, patiently waiting on me. Sanctification is an embracing of all that God is, acknowledging that we are only holding a small piece of the whole of God. God is so big. To try to describe God and His holiness with our earthly words and our earthly minds is futile. Yet, God invites us into that sacredness. He is waiting for us. When we choose to participate in the sacredness of who God is, we realize God has hidden Himself in each one of us. What a mysterious, holy God we serve.

Sanctification is tough though. It is its own process, its own journey. In order to understand it, I think it is best to define the word.

By definition, sanctification is;

> "an act of sanctifying
>
> 2a : the state of being sanctified

---

[82] Thomas Merton, New Seeds of Contemplation, 39–41.

b : the state of growing in divine grace as a result of Christian commitment after baptism or conversion"[83]

That seems about as clear as mud, but if we drill down, we see the word "sanctify;"

"sanctifying" means:

"to set apart to a sacred purpose or to religious use; consecrate

2. to free from sin; purify

3a: to impart or impute sacredness, inviolability, or respect to

3b. to give moral or social sanction to

4. to make productive of holiness or piety ·observe the day of the sabbath, to sanctify it"[84]

If sanctification is "the act of sanctifying", and sanctifying is "to be set apart for a sacred purpose" and is also "a state of growing in divine grace as a result of Christian commitment," then let us take one important step and look at grace.

Grace is:

"1a. unmerited divine assistance given to humans for their regeneration or sanctification

b. a virtue coming from God

c. a state of sanctification enjoyed through divine assistance[85]"

Grace is "divine assistance given to humans for sanctification." Divine assistance (help) offered by the divine (God) given to us (humans) for

---

[83] https://www.merriam-webster.com/dictionary/sanctification

[84] https://www.merriam-webster.com/dictionary/sanctifying

[85] https://www.merriam-webster.com/dictionary/grace

sanctification or sacredness imparted to us by God. God set us apart for His purposes. God plans to help us with this sacredness. We have been set apart for God's purposes. With God's help, His sacredness will be given to us. Wow!

Do you know how special you are? And not just you, all of us. We cannot get where we are going on our own. It is all part of a divine plan. Our Maker wants to help us get there. It is only through God's help that we obtain our holiness. We have been set apart because we are God's. Plain and simple. God created us. He placed His image inside of us, the same one that Christ carried. I thought my level of commitment to my discipleship would lead me to sanctification. The only thing I need to be committed to is God.

Looking over my years of church service, I realize I was working hard. I never stopped to ask myself why, or why I even wanted to be sanctified. I always associated sanctification with knowledge. You know the old saying, "knowledge is power." With the ego at work, my desire for holiness was nothing more than a power play. All my attempts of perfecting Christ through discipleship and service were weak efforts of the ego's hunger.

Sanctification is not about knowledge. If it is, it is the knowledge of who God is and who God is in me. Once we encounter God, we are aware of God's holiness. In the sacredness of those moments with God, God makes us holy. You cannot work to be sanctified. It just comes naturally by being with God.

As God draws us into Himself, God begins the work of sanctification. The drawing and the sanctifying go hand in hand, just like faith and works.[86] "Every time you draw into God, God draws into you,"[87] you

---

[86] James Chapter 2 NIV

experience God and are changed. By being with God, you begin to think, feel, and respond differently. Should we long for sanctification? I am not sure. What I do know is that when you come into the presence of God, God changes you. You are coming into holiness. The fake-self shrinks back, allowing the true self to emerge. In being with God, I not only find God, I find my true self.

Thomas Merton explains how being with God is the only way back to our true selves. He relates finding our identity to finding our sanctity, and how it is only through God that it can be obtained. In his book, *New Seeds of Contemplation*, he writes,

> "We can be ourselves or not, as we please . . . We may be true or false, the choice is ours . . .
>
> Our vocation is not simply to be, but to work together with God in the creation of our own life, our own identity, our own destiny. We are free beings . . . The secret of my full identity is hidden in Him. He alone can make me who I am . . .
>
> The seeds that are planted in my liberty at every moment, by God's will, are the seeds of my own identity, my own reality, my own happiness, my own sanctity.
>
> To refuse them is to refuse everything; it is the refusal of my own existence and being: of my identity, my very self."[88]

---

1. **Think about God and the holiness of God. List all the words you can think of to describe God and HIS holiness.**

---

[87] James Chapter 4 NIV
[88] Thomas Merton, New Seeds of Contemplation, 31–33.

Jumpstart:

This is a free-writing exercise. Take a moment and think about God. Close your eyes, breathe in for three counts and hold it, letting it out slowly. Do this for three cycles. What do you see? Open your eyes and begin writing every word that pops into your mind or whatever you saw. Reflect on what you have written. Compare your response to your reflections in **Chapter One, question 1, Jumpstart**. How have your thoughts changed?

Just the Facts:

- **Psalm 77:13 CEB;** God, your way is holiness!

    Who is as great a god as you, God?

- **Psalm 147:5 NIV;** Great is our Lord and mighty in power;

    his understanding has no limit.

- **1 Peter 2:9 The Passion;** But you are God's chosen treasure—priests who are kings, a spiritual "nation" set apart as God's devoted ones. He called you out of darkness to experience his marvelous light, and now he claims you as his very own. He did this so that you would broadcast his glorious wonders throughout the world.

2. **Think of the most sacred of all your experiences with God. Journal the experience here. How were you changed by the experience?**

Jumpstart:

Think about my story of God asking me to pray for the woman's knee. Think about God giving me a second chance to pray with her. Think about the healing she received through the act of obedience. What might God be calling you to do?

Just the Facts:

- **Numbers 14:18 CEB;** The Lord is very patient and absolutely loyal, forgiving wrongs and disloyalty.

- **John 6:44 ESV;** No one can come to me unless the Father who sent me draws him. And I will raise him up on the last day.

- **Matthew 5:14-16 The Message;** You're here to be light, bringing out the God-colors in the world. God is not a secret to be kept. We're going public with this, as public as a city on a hill. If I make you light-bearers, you don't think I'm going to hide you under a bucket, do you? I'm putting you on a light stand. Now that I've put you there on a hilltop, on a light stand—shine! Keep an open house; be generous with your lives. By opening up to others, you'll prompt people to open up with God.

- **1 John 4:12 ESV;** . . . if we love one another, God abides in us and his love is perfected in us.

3. **As you think about God, list all the times you experienced God. Are there times you may have experienced God but did not realize it? How does that make you feel? Think about sharing your story with someone.**

THE ME DISEASE

Jumpstart:

I remember sitting on my porch swing with my eyes closed. I could feel a light breeze rustling through my hair. The sun began to warm my face as the birds chirped. I felt the presence of God and knew I was not alone. Basking in the goodness of God's creation, I began to understand that God is in creation. God changed me that day, and I found a new appreciation for trees, grass, birds, and nature.

Just the Facts:

- **Romans 1:20 NLT;** For ever since the world was created, people have seen the earth and sky. Through everything God made, they can clearly see his invisible qualities—his eternal power and divine nature. So they have no excuse for not knowing God.

- **Philippians 1:6 CEB;** I'm sure about this: the one who started a good work in you will stay with you to complete the job by the day of Christ Jesus.

- **Lamentations 3:21-23 NIV;** Yet this I call to mind and therefore I have hope:
Because of the Lord's great love we are not consumed, for his compassions never fail. They are new every morning; great is your faithfulness.

- **John 1:3 NIV;** Through him all things were made; without him nothing was made that has been made.

- **Job 12:7-12 The Message;** But ask the animals what they think—let them teach you;
let the birds tell you what's going on.

Put your ear to the earth—learn the basics.
Listen—the fish in the ocean will tell you their stories.
Isn't it clear that they all know and agree
that God is sovereign, that he holds all things in his hand—
Every living soul, yes,
every breathing creature?
Isn't this all just common sense,
as common as the sense of taste?
Do you think the elderly have a corner on wisdom,
that you have to grow old before you understand life?

Prayer: Holy God, Lord of Power and Might, the heavens proclaim the work of your hands, the sky rejoices in all that you are. We are your people, the product of your handiwork. Open our eyes that we might see how sacred you are. Open our minds so we might understand how great you are. Open our hearts so we might know how much you love us. Thank you for drawing us in, perfecting Christ in us. Thank you that I can experience you in so many ways; in others, in nature, in myself. Let me experience you more. In Jesus' name, Amen.

Chapter Twelve

We are ONE
The Joy of Community

As OUR JOURNEY TOGETHER IS nearing its end, I feel we are really at the beginning of something more. There is a oneness emerging, a sense of community. Community does not have to be a group or organization. I mean, it can be. People find community in all sorts of places. Churches, civic groups, book clubs, hunt clubs, Moms in Prayer groups. These are all great places to find community. But there are surprise places community exists, like; a group of alumni that continue to live life together after graduation, supper clubs, AA meetings, hospice grief groups, or the local soup kitchen. When we come together and share our lives with each other on a regular basis, community is created. Even in the writing of this book, I believe we are forming a new community.

One of the best things that happens in community is sharing. Acts 2:42-47 CEB talks about this coming together:

> "The believers devoted themselves to the apostles' teaching, to the community, to their shared meals, and to their prayers. A sense of awe came over everyone. God performed many wonders

and signs through the apostles. All the believers were united and shared everything. They would sell pieces of property and possessions and distribute the proceeds to everyone who needed them. Every day, they met together in the temple and ate in their homes. They shared food with gladness and simplicity. They praised God and demonstrated God's goodness to everyone. The Lord added daily to the community those who were being saved."

In their coming together and sharing, they created community. On top of that, they devoted themselves to the teachings, becoming disciples, sharing meals, and praying for one another. When we come together in unity and share, we experience God. By participating in community, we support each other and bear each other's burdens.[89] When one suffers, we all suffer, and we rejoice when one rejoices.[90] Find community and you will find God. Find God and you will be led to community.

I have a group of friends that gets together on a regular basis for the sole purpose of eating. A lot of life can be shared across the dining room table. Whether we know it or not, we stumbled into our own little community. Because we have been friends for so long, we have been able to celebrate marriages, careers, our kids, holidays, and just being together.

One of our favorite things to do is prepare the meal together. We make and bake and talk and laugh. We share and care and sometimes cry. We have lived our lives together, often through the preparation of our dinner. Even the kids help in the kitchen, preparing smoked salmon and cream cheese roll-ups and stuffed jalapeno poppers. Everyone has a job, and everyone brings something to the table. We experience great joy in being together.

---

[89] Galatians 6:2 ESV
[90] 1 Corinthians 12:26 ESV

Through telling old tales and sharing new stories, I realize that when one of us is happy, we share in their happiness. But, when one of us is sad, we are also sad. We not only share a meal, we bear each other's burden, often comforting one another with support or a shoulder to cry on. At the end of the evening, we share in the cleanup, sending everyone home with leftovers. This is one of the most joyful things I do. We stumbled onto community and somehow found God in the process. I realize it is not about me, but we. We are one, collectively. When one suffers, we all suffer. When one rejoices, we all rejoice. This is the 'me2WE' God has been revealing to me.

Me2We

That All May Be One. John 17:21

Logo created by Julie Wooten

Shifting into this "me2We" mentality, I understand that we have been created for community. As God draws and sanctifies us, we experience His love and we are changed. God then sends us back out into community to be that love for other people. Living in community, we act as the body of Christ, which is the kingdom of God on Earth. We are that kingdom.

Jesus talks about this oneness in John 17:20-23 ESV when he says,

> ". . . that they may all be one, just as you, Father, are in me, and I in you . . ."

Jesus longs for us to be one, just as he and God are one. When we come together, we see a clearer picture of who God is and experience the fullness of God. I see God in me and experience God in you. Maybe this is what Jesus is referring to when he speaks of making our joy complete.

There is a sharing of this sanctity, a sharing of this oneness. But if God sets me apart and leaves you out, where does that leave us? In some exclusive club where no one knows who is in and who is out? God does not work that way. God is love and all God can be is love. Love includes us all and makes us whole. Love is all of us coming together in one accord.

We see this love demonstrated through God the Father and God the Son. Even before Jesus' death, he modeled what a relationship with God looks like. In John 17, Jesus loved us so much, that he prayed for us before we were ever here. The gravity of this act for me, a future believer, fell on me one day.

I have read this passage numerous times, never grasping the greatness of what Jesus is doing for us. I never understood how much he loved us even before we were here. The day I finally got it, I was overwhelmed with emotion at the thought of Jesus himself praying for me. And, not just me, all of us. The great love God and Son have for us is overwhelming.

In the passage, Jesus longs for our joy to be complete. In order to receive the full measure, we have to recognize that we, being just like Jesus, carry the divine image inside of us. This recognition gives us a new appreciation for one another. We are one, sharing the divine image of God. You have the divine image of God within you. I have the divine image of God within me. When we come together, our joy is made complete. It is our oneness of God's image that enables us to receive the full measure of Christ's joy.

As we continue in John 17, Jesus asks God to sanctify us by God's truth. This is the word of God. God has given us the scriptures which tell us everything we need to know about God, creation, love, and relationship. God also gave us Jesus to model this relationship. Jesus shows us what a relationship with the Divine looks like. You can read all the stories in scripture, but this is head knowledge. We need the heart knowledge. Praise the Lord, we already know with God's divine assistance, God will do what God needs to do. We only need to participate.

First, acknowledge I am a child of God and God's spirit lives within me. Second, when we confess with our mouths that Jesus is Lord and believe in our hearts,[91] that divine spirit, the true self, comes alive. Like a flash, head knowledge becomes heart knowledge. God invades our very being and is no longer something we have read about; now we know God. Everything changes.

Once I begin living out of the heart knowledge, out of my true self, I realize it is not about me. I am part of something bigger. It is about us. This unspeakable joy I have found, I want to share, drawing me into community. In our coming together, we are made complete. Separate we are nothing. But together, we are the kingdom of God here on Earth.

In Jesus' sanctification, He sanctified the whole, making us a part of something bigger than ourselves. Jesus followed the path, unclear of where he was going. He chose to go anyway. He chose to participate. In those last moments of Jesus' life, He cried out, "My God, my God, why have you forsaken me."[92] Even before He went to the cross, He pleaded with God to take the cup from Him but ended with "not my will but yours be done."[93] He surrendered His will to the will of the Father. Because of his obedience, we all can rejoice today. It was only through divine assistance Jesus could have died the death that saved us all. God

---

[91] Romans 10:9
[92] Matthew 27:46 NIV
[93] Luke 22:42 NIV

was with Him even though Jesus did not know it. Trusting God, Jesus was obedient even unto death.

Thomas Merton says,

> ". . . when you realize that the only thing worth living for is sanctity. Then you will be satisfied to let God lead you to sanctity by paths that you cannot understand . . ."[94]

When God asked us to sell our house, I felt like I was being led down a path I did not understand. That act of obedience led to God asking us to sell my business to follow a dream of writing a book. By the world's standards, my business was successful. It not only provided for me and my family, but four other employees and their families. Why would I sell it to chase after a dream? But hearing, trusting, and obeying God set us on a path we did not fully understand. Being obedient to what God had called us to do, we continued. We sold our house, left our church, and sold my business. Each one was a task unto itself, teaching us new lessons of who God is in our lives. We had no idea that first act of obedience in selling our house would open the way for us to sell my business and write this book. The joy we have experienced has been unspeakable.

Still, I get hung up on questions like, "How much farther?" and "When will we get there?" Fortunately, God is still teaching us, showing us the importance of our relationship with Him. By participating in what God asks of us, we demonstrate our trust, knowing that God has our best interests in mind. It has not been easy, but the rewards far outweigh any discomfort. Every step we take in faith, God meets us and hands us whatever we need next. The greatest blessing is the love of God we have found, not only in ourselves, but in each other. Oh, the lessons I have learned when I chose to participate.

---

[94] Thomas Merton, New Seeds of Contemplation, 40.

The great thing about being in community with one another is we get to live out our faith and practice relationships, including forgiveness. When we can come together in our differences, we see God's love in action. Every "us" is a small community.

Practicing forgiveness is difficult. When someone hurts my feelings, am I brave enough to admit it in a loving way? Not in a defensive attack mode? We must go in love and vulnerability, confessing our hurt. When I react to the pain, I hurt the other person. The fake-self encourages me to retaliate. People who have been hurt, or are currently hurting, often hurt other people. God's way is love and to respond in love. When we move into our true self, we begin to respond in healthy ways that heal, not hurt.

The other day, I was on the phone with a friend, sharing some exciting news. Instead of her being happy for me, she began to question me. Offended by her response, I shut down, ending the conversation and the call. Realizing she hurt my feelings, she sent me a text apologizing. I acknowledged her apology by text, but it did not make me feel any better. If she were talking with me, she might have heard in my tone that something was still wrong.

After her apology, my fake-self convinced me it would be best to avoid her. This is a maneuver I have used for years. Unhealthy as it is, I did it anyway, knowing if enough time passed, my feelings would diminish, and I could act as if it never happened.

Halfway through the week, while writing my blog, a bright orange sticky note caught my eye. It was a thought I had scribbled down some time back. The note read, "As long as we avoid the uncomfortable, we will never grow to be who we were created to be." I felt God nudging me to call my friend. I rolled my eyes, pushing the note and the idea out of my head.

THE ME DISEASE

That night, watching a rerun of my favorite NYC cop drama, I listened to the TV grandpa tell his grandson these profound words, "The conversation you are avoiding is the very one you need to have." Again, I felt God inviting me to participate in this work. I did not want to have the conversation. I knew as long as I avoided the uncomfortable, I would never grow to who God created me to be.

A whole week went by before I decided to call my friend. I didn't intend to mention the incident. She did most of the talking, bringing me up to speed on some drama in her life. As I listened, she began to tell me about a friend who had hurt her feelings. I was amazed at the similarities as she admitted to avoiding the person. I explained to her if we were healthy people, we could go in love, and admit to the person how we were feeling. This is where forgiveness happens.

As the words rolled off my tongue, the tears filled my eyes. God was inviting me again to participate in His work. With an open door, it was up to me whether I would walk through it. I squirmed, wanting to be brave enough to admit she had hurt my feelings. As our conversation drew to a close, I took a deep breath, knowing it was now or never. I was honest with her, admitting she had hurt my feelings. Forgiveness was ours that day, and our friendship is stronger because of it.

We either have the hard conversation in love, or our relationships suffer. When one of us suffers, we all suffer. This is community. God is continuing to teach me. Learn the lessons or you will keep having to learn the same lesson. Love well, be courageous enough to have the hard conversation, in person or at least voice-to-voice. In these moments, we find forgiveness, reconciliation, healing and more love. There is always more love.

Recently, my small community of friends faced their own tragedy. Strangely enough, I have a better understanding of community as we grieve alongside them. As they suffer, we suffer, too. We ache for our friends in pain. We want to help them, to fix it or make it all better. Nothing we do will make it go away.

When we choose to stand with others in their pain, we carry God's love into that situation. God is in us, therefore when we walk into a room, God comes with us. I have experienced so much of God's love during times of grief. It is as if the bigger the pain, the more love God has to offer. I don't really understand it. Even still, as a community, we are called to bear each other's burdens. Often, our presence is the only gift we have to give.

Somehow, by standing in the gap of others' loss, we give them hope. I heard a chaplain say, "The great thing about God is that the door is always open." It's a mystery really, how God's love pours out into every part of our lives. God is here. Even in all this pain, God is with us. When we don't even know it, God is the one carrying us through our darkest days. Often it is the love from others, our community, that helps us carry on.

This morning as I sit on my swing, I close my eyes and reflect on God and His goodness. I am thankful God allows me to participate in His love and mercy. As the sun warms my face, I realize God is everywhere, in everything. Even in my breath, God is here, in this moment.

My mind wanders to a future me. I catch glimpses of her from time to time, adorned with little more than hope and determination. There she is, emerging from within. To deny her, this new me, would be denying my true self. Yet, I don't quite know who I am. But every day, I am one step closer. It will not be a great reveal. No, this is a glorious unfolding. Little fragments of clarity and lessons learned knock away at the fake-self, drawing me closer to my true self.

With my eyes still closed, I take another breath, as my swing sways gently back and forth. I can see myself, standing before me. The pendulum of my mind keeps me in a state of flux, clinging to past regrets and unknown futures. Back and forth it swings, robbing me of the most important state of all. The now.

There is power in the breath, and it holds me here in this moment. I see me, standing before myself. I do an Asian bow, eyes closed, head to hands, hands to heart, humbly and respectfully bent to my higher self. I silently surrender and let go. The bowed-self vanishes, leaving only my true self behind. Suspended in the breath, I know I am exactly where I am supposed to be. This is me. This is now.

My prayer for you is that you have not only glimpsed God through my stories, but that you are experiencing God in your own life. God has gifted us with life and with each other. We are to learn from one another, to be together, and to see God in each other. God loves us so much that He was willing to give everything for our sake.

I want to leave you with this. Genesis 1:27 reads, "God created man in his own image, in the image of God he created him; male and female he created them." I let the words guide me as I meditate over the text. The word "man" jumps out at me and I associate it with "Adam" and "Adam" with 'humanity'. The definition of "man" is "an individual human, humankind, the history of man." When I look at 'humankind,' I find "humanity." Do you know what the definition of 'humanity' is? I was surprised to read, "compassionate, sympathetic, or generous; the quality of state of being." These are the qualities of God.

As I reread the scripture, the word "created" pops out at me and I search the definition. Created means "To make or bring into existence something new". Again, I go back to the scripture and run my finger by every word. The word "image" jumps out and is defined as "a visual representation of something." And there it is. God brought us into existence to be "a visual representation of Himself." Confirming everything I know to be true, I know who we are and who God created us to be.

In *Immortal Diamond*, Richard Rohr relates this very thought in this way:

> "Your True Self is who you are, and always have been in God, and at its core, it is love itself. Love is both who you are and who you are still becoming, like a sunflower seed that becomes its own sunflower. Most of human history has called the True Self your "soul" or "your participation in the eternal life of God." The great surprise and irony is that 'you,' or who you think you are, have nothing to do with its original creation, or its demise. It's sort of disempowering and utterly empowering at the same time, isn't it? All you can do is nurture it, which is saying quite a lot. It is love becoming love in this unique form called 'me.'"

We are the visual representation of God. Let that thought settle on you like a warm blanket on a cold night. We are love because God is love. Love is becoming love in this vessel called me; put us all together, and you have the "me2We."

---

1. **Think of a time when you experienced community. How did that feel? Where are other places that you can experience community?**

Jumpstart:

In helping at a local soup kitchen, I have met several folks that help serve the meals, organize the meals, and receive the meals. Sometimes, I help in the kitchen, sometimes I serve the plates, and sometimes I sit and eat with the folks. I found community at the soup kitchen. Sitting and eating with people allows me to get to know them. I met a kind man who has been coming to eat at this kitchen for the last 10 years. He is about 74 and has been coming since before I started helping. I love to sit at his table. I feel accepted and loved. I encourage you to get to know people. You may discover community in the most unlikely of places.

Just the Facts:

- **Matthew 18:20 ESV;** For where two or three are gathered in my name, there am I among them.

- **John 15:13 CEB;** No one has greater love than to give up one's life for one's friends.

- **John 13:34 NLT;** I am giving you a new commandment: Love each other. Just as I have loved you, you should love each other.

- **1 Timothy 6:18 AMP;** Instruct them to do good, to be rich in good works, to be generous, willing to share with others.

- **Psalm 133:1 NIV;** How good and pleasant it is when God's people live together in unity!

- **Hebrews 10:24-25 NIV;** And let us consider how to stir up one another to love and good works, not neglecting to meet together, as is the habit of some, but encouraging one another . . .

2. **Have you ever suffered when others suffered or rejoiced when others rejoice? What does it mean to bear one another's burdens? Is there something God has been asking you to participate in? What could you do today to choose to participate in that work?**

Jumpstart:

How many times has God nudged you to do, say, or read something? I hope by sharing my stories you may see God at work in your own life. Reflect on a time when you felt God nudging you to do something.

Just the Facts:

- **Galatians 6:2 ESV;** Bear one another's burdens, and so fulfill the law of Christ.

- **Colossians 3:14 NIV;** And over all these virtues put on love, which binds them all together in perfect unity.

- **1 John 1:7 CEB;** if we live in the light in the same way as he is in the light, we have fellowship with each other, and the blood of Jesus, his Son, cleanses us from every sin.

- **Matthew 5:16 The Message;** Here's another way to put it: You're here to be light, bringing out the God-colors in the world. God is not a secret to be kept. We're going public with this, as public as a city on a hill. If I make you light-bearers, you don't think I'm going to hide you under a bucket, do you? I'm putting you on a light stand. Now that I've put you there on a hilltop, on a light stand—shine! Keep open house; be generous with your lives. By opening up to others, you'll prompt people to open up with God, this generous Father in heaven.

3. **Think of a time you experienced immeasurable joy. Journal about that experience. Where did you experience that joy? Were you able to share that joy with others? What was that like?**

THE ME DISEASE

Jumpstart:

Start a gratitude journal, listing out all the things you are thankful for. Listen to the Hillsong song, "So Will I." Journal your thoughts of God, you, and God in you. How can you say "yes" to who God created you to be?

Just the Facts:

- **Psalm 16:11 NIV;** You make known to me the path of life; you will fill me with joy in your presence, with eternal pleasures at your right hand.

- **Isaiah 61:10 ESV;** I will greatly rejoice in the Lord;
  my soul shall exult in my God,
  for he has clothed me with the garments of salvation;
  he has covered me with the robe of righteousness . . .

- **John 16:24 CEB;** Up to now, you have asked nothing in my name. Ask and you will receive so that your joy will be complete.

- **1 Peter 1:8-9 NIV;** Though you have not seen him, you love him; and even though you do not see him now, you believe in him and are filled with an inexpressible and glorious joy, for you are receiving the end result of your faith, the salvation of your souls.

Prayer: Father God, Creator of the Heavens and Earth and all of humanity, thank you for what you have done for us. Thank you for the life you have given us. Thank you that you invite us to participate in the work you are doing here on Earth. Thank you that you are love, and out of that love, you created us. Thank you that we are the exact representation of You. Help us to realize that truth, and share it with the world. In Jesus' Name, Amen.

*May the God of hope
fill you with all joy and peace
as you trust in Him,
so that you may overflow with hope
by the power of the Holy Spirit.*[95]

---

[95] Romans 15:13 NIV

Check Me out on Facebook, Twitter, Instagram and LinkedIn.

Check out my website at:
www.MelissaHThompson.com

Subscribe to my weekly inspirational blog at:
www.MelissaHThompson.com

Contact me for speaking engagements,
small group studies and book clubs at:
melissa@melissahthompson.com

Be on the lookout for more of my books:
OTHERS
and
The Disciplines

Also, my husband Travis Thompson's new book:
Following Her, Following God

SELF-PUBLISHING SCHOOL

NOW IT'S YOUR TURN

Discover the EXACT 3-step blueprint you need to become a bestselling author in 3 months.

Self-Publishing School helped me, and now I want them to help you with this FREE WEBINAR!

Even if you're busy, bad at writing, or don't know where to start, you CAN write a bestseller and build your best life.

With tools and experience across a variety of niches and professions, Self-Publishing School is the only resource you need to take your book to the finish line!

DON'T WAIT

Watch this FREE WEBINAR now, and Say "YES" to becoming a bestseller:

https://xe172.isrefer.com/go/affegwebinar/bookbrosinc7391/

Made in the USA
Columbia, SC
15 September 2022